CONTROL OF WORKING CAPITAL

A programme of management priorities

CONTROL OF WORKING CAPITAL

A programme of management priorities

Edited by Martin Grass

Contributions by W V Adams, A G Jones,
P H A Kenyon, A B Thomas

Gower Press

First published in Britain in 1972 by Gower Press Limited
Epping, Essex

Set in 10 on 12 pt Times Roman and printed in England by
A Wheaton and Co Ltd, Exeter

Contents

Illustrations

Preface

This book defines working capital as stocks and debtors less trade creditors. Working capital thus defined, together with fixed assets, comprises the operating assets of a business.

Mismanagement, i.e. the uncontrolled over-expansion of working capital, has caused many businesses to fail; and in less severe cases has stunted their growth. Yet how many businesses look at working capital in this light and attempt to control it?

Control of Working Capital is the first book to examine systematically the structure of this task by setting out practical management guidelines, in the knowledge that this is a task dispersed among several business functions. The book is unsophisticated and in academic terms incomplete: it singles out priorities for action. The manager, let it be said, is obliged to concentrate on priorities.

The contributors wrote a specific section or group of sections each. The text was subsequently edited to give it a reasonable degree of uniformity of approach.

Much in the early sections was provided by two senior managers of the Plessey Company. Alec Jones, then Financial Control and Analysis Executive, and now with Plessey Alloys Corporation (USA), wrote on the management control of working capital; Alfred Kenyon, Plessey's Treasurer, wrote on the sources and best use of funds. Bill Adams, Credit Manager with Mullard Limited, contributed the section on trade debtors and material on the financing of exports. Adin Thomas, Management Services Manager at Ferodo Limited, wrote the chapters on the contribution of stock control to working capital.

The text was edited into its final shape by Martin Grass, editor of *Accountant's Week*, who wrote in a number of introductory and bridging sections.

Introduction

Shortage of funds for working capital has been possibly the biggest cause of business failures in recent years. New ventures fail for lack of continuing finance: others are forever postponed. However, these are minor disappointments compared to the total collapse of major companies which has been brought about by the drying up of funds required for day-to-day running of the enterprise.

Two of the most celebrated victims of working capital shortages—Rolls-Royce and Upper Clyde Shipbuilders—illustrate the seriousness of the management problem and the need for priority action. In spite of an international reputation for technological excellence, the best brand name in the world and a continuing history of reported profitability, Rolls-Royce could not survive when the money ran out. The Upper Clyde Shipbuilders failure demonstrated that working capital was a more pressing priority than full order books and notable advances in productivity and industrial relations. The experience of these world-famous companies has been mirrored by all too many medium and smaller sized firms.

The need for skilled working capital management will, if anything, become greater in the future. Part of the problem is the total supply of money and credit available to companies and in recent years both Labour and Conservative governments have used the supply of credit as a method of regulating the economy. In particular, the restriction of credit is now a primary weapon in the struggle to control inflation.

The securement of adequate funds and the application of these funds is a general management responsibility. It cannot be left to the company's accountant or finance department since it involves policy decisions affecting all the management functions: production, marketing, and administration. Skilful working capital management requires an overall plan approved and applied by all the senior management. This book is an attempt to provide the concepts and the techniques which will make such planning and action effective.

The structure of the book is determined by the priorities in working capital management. The first requirement is to ensure that there is a system for management control and this is described in Chapter 2. The forecasting of requirements for funds and the sources of finance for working capital are studied in Chapters 3, 4 and 5, in particular the methods of obtaining short-term loans and of acquiring the maximum credit from suppliers.

The most pressing and persistent need for working capital funds in business is to meet the investment in debtors and trading stock. It is their nature to increase as business expands and to increase still further in response to inflation. In Chapters 6 and 7 the policy and management of trade debtors is detailed in such a way as to indicate how trade can be expanded without extending unnecessary credit to customers. In Chapters 8, 9, 10 and 11 similar procedures are given for the management of stocks.

Finally, special aspects of working capital management which apply to exporting are considered in Part 5. Methods of export financing are briefly described in Chapter 12, while the remaining chapters deal with management of export debtors and specific risks involved in export selling.

Some practical suggestions for managements which find themselves with a surplus of liquidity are put forward in Appendix 1, and the methods of avoiding shortfall directions for private companies are described in Appendix 2.

Part One

The Place of Working Capital in the Business

The Importance of Working Capital

Working capital defined

Like many other financial terms, the expression "working capital" is used in different senses by different people. Strictly speaking, all capital supplied by shareholders and creditors to a business enterprise "works" by earning revenues, providing finance for expansion, being invested in new assets and used up in discharging obligations incurred in the course of everyday operations.

However, a large proportion of the available funds is normally invested in fixed assets, such as land, buildings, plant and equipment, which for obvious reasons cannot be easily reconverted into cash.

The concept of "working capital" is associated with current assets, which include cash, near-cash (eg short-term securities) and trading non-monetary assets such as stocks, work-in-progress and debtors. A proportion of funds required for investment in these assets is provided by suppliers and short-term creditors, while the remainder—the difference between the total current assets and the total current liabilities—must be financed from permanent capital.

Working capital, therefore, can be defined as the net balance of current operating assets or the surplus of current assets over current liabilities. This is a usual standard definition, but in this book we shall use a somewhat narrower concept of working capital as the net sum of stocks and debtors *less* creditors and advance payments on contracts. The latter are an important feature in contract work.

A balance sheet is a static picture of net assets employed in a company, and how they are financed, at a given point in time. Figure 1:1 is a balance sheet drawn up so that it shows working capital as defined in this book.

	£	£
NET ASSETS EMPLOYED		
Fixed assets		
Land and buildings	5 000	
Plant and equipment	3 000	
Motor vehicles	500	
		8 500
Working capital		
Stocks and work-in-progress	3 000	
Trade debtors and prepayments	9 000	
Less creditors and accrued expenses	(6 000)	
		6 000
		14 500
Less		
Taxation	1 600	
Proposed dividend	500	
		2 100
		12 400
NET ASSETS		
FINANCED BY		
Shareholders' funds		
Issued share capital	5 000	
Reserves and surplus	4 000	
		9 000
Long-term borrowing		2 000
Overdrafts	1 400	
Short-term borrowing	1 000	
Short-term investments	(700)	
Cash in hand	(300)	
		1 400
Net liquid position		
		12 400
NET FUNDS		

FIGURE 1:1   BALANCE SHEET AT 30 JUNE 1971

Working capital and management objectives

In a period of tight money supply and credit restrictions, the amount of finance required for efficient operations, planned expansion and profitable investments is a critical factor in the management of company funds.

The management's task is to strike a balance between the retention of liquid funds and a minimum investment in working capital in accordance with the following objectives:

1 To keep stocks and debtors at the lowest possible level consistent with the efficient operation of the business. A chronic shortage of stock or an unwillingness to extend the usual credit terms to customers could seriously hinder the running of the company.
2 To obtain the largest possible amount of credit that the suppliers are willing to grant, consistent with optimum buying principles.

Exceptionally, these general rules may be subject to some modifications in the case of prosperous private limited companies, which are faced with special taxation problems. This situation is described in more detail in Appendix 2.

The responsibility for achieving these objectives cannot be confined to the company's accountant since, as this book will show, the management of the working capital involves major policy decisions not only in the finance department, but also in the production and marketing areas.

Hence, it is essential for the company's senior executives as well as line managers and their staff to become actively involved in the control of working capital and to understand the effects of major changes in the company's stocks, debtors and creditors.

All such changes should be either planned or anticipated, so that the flow of funds is as smooth as possible, bottlenecks and undue delays are avoided and additional finance—whether derived from internal operations or obtained from outside sources—is available when needed.

Management can determine the level of working capital by planned changes in its component parts or in the total funds employed in the concern. Some of these changes, which will be described in more detail in the following chapters, are illustrated in Figure 1:2. In column *A*, the company proposes to increase its liquidity by raising additional loans or issuing more share capital. Its ability to do so depends on various factors, such as the security available and the prospects of earning profits. It should be recognised that:

(a) Both methods are costly
(b) Share capital is permanent
(c) Loans may be for any length of time

POSITION NOW			PROPOSED CHANGES		
			A	B	C
Fixed assets		60	60	20	60
Current assets					
Stock	30		30	30	60
Debtors	20		20	20	30
	50				
Cash*	—		40	40	—
	50		90	90	90
Less current liabilities					
Creditors	10		10	10	50
	40		80	80	40
Working capital		40	80	80	40
Total net operating assets		100	140	100	100
Current ratio		5:1	9:1	9:1	1.8:1
Liquid ratio		2:1	6:1	6:1	0.6:1

FIGURE 1:2   WORKING CAPITAL AS A SECTION OF TOTAL FUNDS

* In this example, cash has been included in "working capital" so as to illustrate the effect of the changes on the current and liquid ratios. Cash is not normally included because cash is the effect rather than the cause of working capital changes.

B: In order to release a proportion of total funds invested in fixed assets, the company may decide to sell some of the assets and manage without them or lease them back from the purchaser. Where fixed assets are wearing out and so reducing in value, the depreciation releases cash which adds to the working capital. Provided the assets are not replaced at the end of their working life or they are substituted by assets acquired on lease, the boost to working capital is permanent.

C: In this case working capital will remain unchanged, but the company will increase its current assets by financing them through a reduction in its liquidity ratio, ie by obtaining more goods on credit. This course of action is beset with dangers, unless the creditors will agree to wait longer for their money.

Working capital and turnover

As mentioned earlier, one of the main objectives of management in the control of the company's liquidity is to maintain the lowest possible ratio of working capital to turnover.

In the absence of significant changes in the nature of a business, turnover will invariably be the major determinant of the level of working capital. This relationship is less stable in the short than in the long term.

If turnover five years ago was half of its present amount, then we could expect to find that the working capital was also about half of its present size. But if last year's turnover was 10 per cent lower, then it does not follow that working capital must also be lower, because in the short term the ratio tends to fluctuate more widely.

There are a number of reasons why working capital need not vary directly with turnover:

1 The level of work-in-progress depends on the length of the manufacturing time-cycle, and therefore on the products and the product mix.

2 Work-in-progress is geared to output at manufacturing cost, not turnover.

3 Work-in-progress is geared to future rather than past output.

4 Finished stock levels depend on commercial factors. *demand*

5 Debtors depend on credit terms and liquidity of customers.

6 Contract debtors and creditors can vary with the incidence of sub-contract problems, retentions, and export finance facilities.

7 Creditors are geared to purchases rather than turnover and can depend on the degree of vertical integration as well as terms.

8 Advance payments can vary according to the mix of the order book between prime contracts and subcontracts and if they are geared to anything, it is future turnover, usually turnover after a considerable period of delay, such as the year after next.

9 Capital expenditure is not likely to be closely correlated with turnover, so that creditors for capital expenditure might also show a poor correlation with turnover.

10 Management efficiency in the control of working capital is liable to fluctuate.

The analysis of published accounts nevertheless supports the view that the ratio of working capital to turnover normally fluctuates only within reasonable limits.

Figure 1:3, taken from the accounts of two public companies, illustrates the importance of this ratio. The data have been disguised by the application of a single arbitrary factor to all figures.

One of the companies (Locap) has a ratio of capital employed to turnover of 35 per cent of which 23 to 26 per cent represents the working capital ratio. The other company (Hicap) has a capital employed of about 100 per cent of turnover, and the working capital ratio accounts for 72 to 75 per cent of this.

	LOCAP		HICAP	
Basic data	1968	1969	1968	1969
Turnover £M	3.2	3.7	1.7	2.2
Capital employed £M	1.2	1.3	1.7	2.2
Capital employed as % of turnover	35.6	35.1	97.6	101.0
Profit before tax £'000	218	339	276	333
Pre-interest margin on turnover	7.5	9.7	16.2	17.7
Pre-interest return on capital employed	21.5	27.6	16.2	17.3
Earnings per share index (1965 = 100)	159	206	123	145
Capital employed analysis (£'000)				
Stocks	619	634	880	1172
Debtors	933	955	627	962
Creditors	(692)	(746)	(276)	(462)
Working capital	860	843	1231	1672
Net fixed assets	407	586	600	730
Taxation accrued	(69)	(101)	(107)	(99)
Dividends accrued	(49)	(32)	(54)	(61)
Capital employed	1149	1296	1670	2242
Working capital/turnover ratios (%)				
Stocks	18.8	17.1	51.4	52.8
Debtors	28.6	25.8	36.6	43.4
Creditors	(21.2)	(20.1)	(16.2)	(20.8)
Working capital	26.2%	22.8%	71.8%	75.4%

FIGURE 1:3   WORKING CAPITAL AND TURNOVER

Locap and Hicap are in the same industry, but Locap makes small bits and pieces while Hicap supplies complete equipments and systems. This accounts for their radically different working capital/turnover ratios. Both companies have a profitability well above average, with margins rising, and in terms of pre-tax profits they are of the same size.

But there the resemblance ends. Hicap's margins are almost twice as high as Locap's but its return on capital employed is only about two thirds of Locap's. The simple explanation is that Locap turns its capital over three times a year to Hicap's once a year. Similarly, although both companies have a good record in profit growth, Locap's earnings per share have doubled in five years, whereas Hicap's have only gone up by 45 per cent. And when it comes to liquidity, the cash flow comparison shows that Hicap's liquidity deteriorated by £421 000 whereas Locap's is practically unchanged by the events of 1969, and that in each case the total change (nil for Locap, £0.42 million for Hicap) is within £20 000 of the working capital movement. In these businesses working capital is the decisive factor in determining liquidity.

	LOCAP	HICAP
Profit before tax	339	333
Tax paid	(65)	(120)
Dividends paid	(77)	(77)
	197	136
Net increase in fixed assets	(179)	(130)
Working capital	17	(441)
Special transactions	(40)	14
Net change in cash/overdrafts	(5)	(421)

FIGURE 1:4   CASH FLOW, 1969 (£'000)

These comparisons show the crucial importance of the working capital/turnover ratio. Let us assume that both companies in the course of the next five years were to double their turnover. In that case we could expect Locap to need a cash injection of 22% of £3.7 million, say £0.8M. Hicap would presumably need 75% of £2.2M = £1¾M. And if Hicap's present turnover were equal to Locap's it would need 75% of £3.7M = £2¾M against Locap's £0.8M. Moreover, Hicap could not hope to make good this drain out of retained profits, the bulk of which are likely to be absorbed by the increase in net fixed assets.

The message from this comparison of two companies can be summed up as follows:

1 If a company has a high working capital to turnover ratio, then this ratio will have a strong influence on its profitability (return on capital employed), its growth potential and its liquidity.

2 One important determinant in a company's working capital ratio is its product range or product mix.

3 The working capital ratio is obviously a key area for the attention of management.

Management Control of Working Capital

Role of line management

Line managers in industry and commerce are not always aware of the vital role they could play in maintaining working capital at a satisfactory level.

They are responsible for a specialised portion of the operations only and may regard the cash position as being completely beyond their control and something for the "centre" or "head office" to worry about.

It is unfortunate that at the centre of many organisations far more attention is given to pure accounting and budgetary control than to cash management and thus to working capital control. Most medium to large organisations in this country operate budgetary control systems through which they attempt to place responsibility for control of revenue and costs down to the lowest level of management. Few companies, however, attempt to decentralise cash management or management of working capital in a similar manner. Even where control of debtors, creditors and stocks is decentralised, rarely does the system delegate full responsibility for cash management to that level. In many companies cash management is a centralised function with divisions or "the line" merely drawing cheques on a central bank account. Line management is, therefore, denied any responsibility for "self-financing" even though self-financed liquidity, like profit, is earned "in the line."

Profit control which is divorced from cash management can be extremely dangerous because the maximisation of profitability can in certain circumstances be inconsistent with optimising liquidity. Thus, a line manager faced with a declining order book or production schedules and reluctant to reduce his labour force for one reason or another, may decide to produce for stock in the knowledge that through recovery of overheads he will be able to achieve, at least partially, his profit budget. The result will be, of course, reasonable profit budget performance but also a significant increase in stocks and a consequent reduction in liquidity. It is essential, therefore, that financial control should be extended to as low a management level as possible. Managers should have responsibility not only for profit control but also liquidity control through decentralised cash management—Figure 2:1 shows how such responsibilities can be expressed in job descriptions.

Guidelines and procedures

Although some of the procedures outlined in this section will be found mainly in medium-to-large organisations, the basic principles of effective management and control of working capital apply to all types and sizes of business.

In order to achieve a balance between profit control on the one hand and optimum liquidity on the other, the following procedures should be introduced:

1 As far as possible each unit should be responsible for its own accounting system, with the capability to prepare balance sheets and monthly "source and application of funds" statements.
2 Cash management should be decentralised with the company centre acting as a banker.
3 To safeguard the corporate position each unit should be given a bank control limit which it should not exceed without central authorisation.
4 An operating control cash limit should be established for each unit, which would be based on a phased "source and application of funds" statement for the financial year and which would include task reductions in working capital levels.
5 Each unit would be charged interest rates by the centre at, say, normal corporate operating rates up to the level of the operating control limit. Penalty rates of interest should be charged if the operating control limits are exceeded. As mentioned above, in no circumstances should a unit exceed its bank control limit.

These guidelines, if followed, would have the effect of integrating each unit into its proper business environment with responsibility not only for profit performance, but also for cash performance.

EXECUTIVE	RESPONSIBILITIES
Managing director	To show genuine and consistent interest in the subject and thus set an example. To establish systems and controls to monitor responsibilities of other executives.
Sales director/manager	To maintain a steady level of sales during seasonal variations. To obtain the shortest possible settlement terms from customers.
Export sales director/manager	To obtain best settlement terms with customers, make special arrangements with bills of exchange, through ECGD, etc
Purchasing officer/manager	To obtain best terms of settlement from suppliers
Production director/manager	To maintain work-in-progress at optimum level. To avoid unnecessary transfer of funds from working capital into plant and machinery
Stock controller Distribution executive Transport manager	To maintain the stock of finished goods at the correct level and to dispatch goods to customers promptly. To avoid unnecessary transfer of funds from working capital into trucks and mechanical handling plant
Goods inwards warehouse manager	To maintain stocks of raw materials at the lowest level consistent with the need to provide continuous supplies to the factory
Credit controller	To keep customers to their agreed settlement terms and to reduce the risk of bad debts
Accountant	To provide control data for other executives and to assist them in making forecasts and preparing budgets. To arrange for short-term investment of temporary surplus of funds

FIGURE 2:1   PEOPLE INVOLVED IN MANAGEMENT OF WORKING CAPITAL

Working capital budgets

No budget system is complete without a budgeted balance sheet which, as with the profit budget, should be phased in line with the division of the financial year into accounting or control periods. The balance sheet will reflect budgeted capital expenditure for the year and objective working capital levels based on individual criteria for each element of working capital. Cash or liquid funds will, of course, be the balancing figure. The method of evaluating the objective levels of stock can vary from a simple method of applying an objective turnover rate to sales to a more sophisticated system where the budget is based on float levels for every individual part to be worked on within the unit. Whatever level of sophistication is used, however, in developing the budget, there should be a corresponding degree of sophistication in the capability to compare actual levels with budget and to highlight and explain the major reasons for variance. In establishing objective levels for stocks the significant factor is the level of production planned for the period *following* that at which stocks are to be measured and not necessarily the level of production preceding that point.

Objective levels for debtors and creditors will be related to phased sales and purchases and will be calculated through the development of objective ratios of debtors and creditors to sales and purchases respectively. Attention must be paid, however, to any special credit arrangements which would invalidate such overall ratios.

In budgeting elements of working capital it is vitally important that a clear distinction be drawn between realistic "objectives" and "targets." It is quite conceivable that extremely difficult targets may be set for individual elements of working capital, which are purposely set at a point just beyond the realistic reach of the manager concerned. However, as a budget must essentially be an evaluation of realistic levels of achievement in the forthcoming period, it must recognise that there will be an off-standard element in any attempt to achieve targets which are overstretching. Any budget built on unrealistic targets is worse than useless. It fails to identify potential trouble spots and will most certainly result in liquidity shortages which could have been foreseen had the budgets been more realistically pitched.

Impact on capital expenditure

One of the major factors in the annual expenditure of any large or medium-sized company, is the amount spent on new facilities. The future prosperity of a company depends to a large extent on the care with which the new facilities are installed, whether those facilities be for new products or for improved efficiency. It is an unfortunate fact, however, that when cash management budgets begin to "bite," the easiest element of expenditure controllable by the manager is his capital spending, and unless carefully watched, there will be a tendency on the part of the manager to counteract any lack of control over working capital levels by a conscious under-spending on new facilities—to the ultimate detriment of the business. This type of manoeuvring can be countered by regular reviews of actual capital expenditure levels compared with budget, and where it becomes apparent that the situation described above exists the operating control limits for cash management purposes should be adjusted accordingly.

Elements of management control

It may now be useful to deal in a little more detail with the control of the individual elements of working capital and the reader is again reminded that in this context we have defined working capital as the net sum of stocks plus debtors *less* creditors.

Inventories

Control of inventories is meaningful only when it is an integral part of a total production and planning control system which ensures that the right parts in the right quantity are in the right place at the right time. In most organisations stocks are divided for control purposes, as follows:

1　Raw materials
2　Work-in-progress
3　Finished goods
4　Consumable stores

As previously indicated, all the above elements of stocks may be budgeted on the basis of turnover factors or by more sophisticated means. It is, however, naive to believe that it is to a company's advantage to minimise its stock holding at all times. Factors such as bulk purchase discounts, production for stock with no specific covering sales orders during slack periods in order to retain a particularly skilled labour force, or in anticipation of a peak demand in the future, are all aspects which should be considered in developing stock budgets or in measuring actual performance against budget. It is, however, important that production for stock (or "stock orders") is closely controlled and this is best done by a policy of approval of such measures at higher management level consistent with the size of the stock order.

An important factor in establishing objective stock levels and in reviewing the actual levels of stock is that of the cost of carrying stocks. A number of studies in the general engineering sector of industry has indicated that the total cost of carrying stocks is about 20 per cent of the inventory cost per annum. This is, therefore, a very significant cost factor in most organisations. Although incremental reductions of stocks will not necessarily result in an annual saving of costs of 20 per cent of such reductions, it is probably true to say that, with overdraft charges currently at a minimum of 6 per cent, the incremental profit effect of reducing stocks is equivalent to an annual rate of about 11 per cent of the cost of the stocks eliminated.

As with revenue or cost control, it is essential that responsibility for specific segments of stocks is identified with specific individuals.

There is some truth in the argument that detailed control of stocks can be extremely expensive, particularly in those industries where large numbers of different parts are handled. However, this is a classic situation for the application of the 80/20 rule whereby almost invariably about 20 per cent in number of the parts handled represent about 80 per cent of total cost. It is therefore on these high-cost parts that control should be concentrated and on which, in particular, more frequent checks such as cyclical inventory takes must be made.

A further important aspect in the financing of stocks is the possibility of attempting to get the customer to finance stock holdings through advance payments and this is particularly the case where the materials to be purchased represent a high proportion of the ultimate sale price. In other words, where conversion costs represent only a very small percentage of the total contract cost, there is a prima facie case for applying to the customer for funds to finance the holding of stocks, particularly where there is an unduly long cycle time and where it is not possible to phase material deliveries in line with the ability of the company to work on those materials.

Debtors

In the case of debtors it is, of course, necessary to have a strong credit control system with clearly defined levels of authority for the establishment of credit levels. It is important, however, that the controls are not so tight that the ability of the company to obtain business is severely inhibited. In this respect every advantage, provided it is economic, should be taken of credit insurance, particularly that offered by the ECGD, and by commercial insurers.

Control of debtors should include a periodical "ageing analysis" of debts to expose those debts which could become doubtful or bad.

Creditors

In the case of creditors it need hardly be said that the maximum permitted credit be taken—only in exceptional circumstances such as the opportunity for buying at favourable prices will a company pay its creditors before the end of the normal period of credit. Furthermore, where there is mutual trading between one company and another, it would again be foolish for one of the companies to allow longer credit than it is taking from that other company, unless there has been some consideration for this, such as pricing advantage.

Long-term contracting

If our business is concerned with, say, the mass production of paper or cardboard cartons for packaging, then most of the elements of working capital can be treated as separate problems. Work-in-progress is probably not a problem at all, as it may amount to a fraction of a day's output. The other items like materials, finished stocks, debtors and creditors are probably substantial, but usually quite separate fields for management action.

But if we are engaged in large-scale construction or systems business, then many of the problems are interconnected. Working capital then is practically identical with the sum of the amounts of money locked up at any one moment in each of the various contracts.

The special features of this type of business are:

1 Work-in-progress will often be the major item, depending on the length of the time-cycle from start to completion.
2 The importance of the payment terms secured from the customer. These terms vary enormously. For example:
(a) 10% down, 80% on each delivery, 5% on handing over, 5% after a year.
(b) 3 × 20% on certification of 25%, 50%, 75% progress in the manufacturer's works, 20% on delivery, 10% on handing over, 10% after a year.
(c) 10% down, 80% against monthly progress certificates, 5% on handing over, 5% after a year.
(d) 10% down, 90% on handing over.

3   The fine print on documentation may be every bit as important in export contracts as the terms themselves. For example, where the customer is to accept bills of exchange, there must be a foolproof way of getting the bills accepted at the right time and against the right documents. Again, if we have substantial payments due on shipment, but if shipment is to be on ships of the customer's nationality, then we should pause to see whether this will delay our cash receipts. There may only be two Ruritanian ships and we may have to wait six months for one of them. If this risk exists, then the contract must specify that delivery to a UK port constitutes constructive delivery.

4   The importance of subcontract terms. Many contracts of this kind involve substantial subcontracts, and the crucial questions are whether we give our subcontractors "as and when" terms, or shorter terms or longer terms than we get from the ultimate customer. A subcontractor will obviously charge a higher price for "as and when" terms because his payment will then depend on risks in which the subcontractor is not directly involved. On the other hand:

(a) There are many subcontractors with virtually independent large pieces of the main contract, performed on site and virtually in technical if not contractual contact with the ultimate customer.

(b) Financing a subcontractor can be more expensive than the premium which he would require for "as and when" terms.

(c) As an inducement, the subcontractor would of course get his share of down payments, progress payments and the like.

The implementation of the contract terms by the supplier also involves special problems not found in other classes of business. Examples of this are:

1   *Progress certification.* This usually means consultants coming into the works to certify how much of the work-in-progress has been completed to date. There have been instances when no progress payments were collected for over a year because the inspecting consultants were unfamiliar with the product and the company had not devoted any thought or preparation to the logistics of getting them acquainted with the product and enquiring into what documentary or visual aids they would require so as to be able to issue their certificates.

2   *Installation work.* Payment is often against the submission of documents showing the installation staff's hours of work and out-of-pocket expenses on site. Installation staff are not naturally motivated towards

paperwork and if no action is taken, they will let arrears pile up. As there is usually a high labour turnover in this section of the labour force, it will take all the longer to catch up if their *successors* are left to complete the documentation.

3 *Follow-up with customers.* There is usually a corresponding indigestion with paperwork at the customer's office when we have submitted documentation, and it is worth lubricating the mechanism by attending upon the staff concerned, finding out their problems and presenting claims in the most helpful manner in the light of what we learn. These are only a few examples of what needs to be done to get the cash collected at the proper time.

To sum up, the control of working capital employed in contracts involves an architectural stage of designing and negotiating the terms and scheduling production, procurement and subcontracts, and an implementation stage at which not only the physical events but also the clerical procedures need to be kept under constant watch so as to ensure the earliest possible collections and the latest possible cash disbursements.

Long- and short-term considerations

It has already been stated above that unless there is a completely integrated financial control system, profit objectives can be in conflict with working capital minimisation and thus optimisation of liquidity. However, short-term action may be necessary to temporarily improve the company's cash position by taking longer credit than normally allowed from suppliers or by running down stocks to a lower level than would normally be regarded as safe. Such measures carry a considerable risk to the company if continued beyond a very short period. Suppliers may refuse to supply, or if they continue to do so, they may attempt to price at a level which would compensate for financing charges. Stocks that have been run down to a dangerously low level could lead to lost custom through poor service or longer than normal delivery periods.

It is therefore essential that liquidity statements in the form of source and application of funds be projected in detail for, say, each month of the current financial year with regular projections being made for 2 to 3 years beyond the end of the current year. If the latter type of forecast is made, on a realistic basis, it should be obvious whether the business is inadequately capitalised for an expanding rate of business, in which event additional external capital may be required.

Part Two
Sources of Funds for Working Capital

3

Forecasting the Flow of Funds

Working capital as part of net operating assets

The management balance sheet in Figure 1:1 on page 4 shows that total net operating assets consist of fixed assets plus working capital less accrued tax and dividends.

Chapter 1 also showed that working capital in any given business tends to bear a reasonably stable relationship with turnover. This is not necessarily the case with fixed assets. Consequently, different methods are required to forecast these two main elements.

Source and applications of funds statement

This type of statement highlights changes in the employment of net assets, and how those changes are financed. Figure 3:1 shows the balance sheet of Figure 1:1 in summarised form and also how it looked a year later. Figure 3:2 is a simple source and applications of funds statement summarising the events of that year for management. The net investment in fixed assets after depreciation rose by £400, and working capital by £2300. Of this £2700, a net amount of £1400 was financed by profits less cash paid out in tax and dividends, leaving £1300 to be financed by financial changes. A statement laid out like this is useful to management, because it segregates the operating changes from the financing changes.

If, during the year, a complete business is bought, then, for management purposes, the balance sheet must be adjusted at 1 January as if the acquisition had taken place that day, before compiling the source and applications of funds statement. This will show any cash paid for

23

the acquisition as an application. Management want to see how the present (combined) business ticks, and this is how they are told.

	1 JANUARY £	31 DECEMBER £	CHANGE £
Fixed assets (net)	8 500	8 900	+400
Working capital	6 000	8 300	+2 300
Taxation	(1 600)	(1 400)	+200
Dividend proposed	(500)	(500)	0
NET OPERATING ASSETS	12,400	15 300	+2 900
FINANCED BY:			
Shareholders' Funds (Note)	9 000	11 650	+2 650
Long-term borrowing	2 000	1 500	−500
Net liquid position	1 400	2 150	+750
NET FUNDS	12 400	15 300	+2 900
Breakdown of liquid position: Liabilities/(Assets)			
Overdrafts	1 400	1 500	+100
Short-term borrowing	1 000	1 000	0
Short-term investments	(700)	—	+700
Cash in hand	(300)	(350)	−50
	1 400	2 150	+750

Note: Shareholders' Funds have risen by £2650, representing profit before tax of £3500 less tax charge of £1400 (£1600 paid less £200 reduction in amount accrued) less dividend of £500 plus increase in share capital and share premium of £1050.

FIGURE 3:1   SUMMARISED BALANCE SHEETS AT TWO DATES

Forecasting liquidity

Suppose the company in Figures 3:1 and 3:2 is looking at the position at 1 January and trying to *forecast* the position at 31 December. How would they set about it? The simplified form of balance sheet and source and applications of funds statement helps to identify the various tasks:

1   Forecast profit before tax
2   Calculate tax and dividend payments

YEAR ENDED 31 DECEMBER

CASH INFLOW /(OUTFLOW)	£	£
Profit before tax (Note 2)	3 500	
Tax paid	(1 600)	
Dividend paid	(500)	
		1 400
Capital expenditure	(1 500)	
Depreciation charged	800	
Book value of fixed assets disposals (Note 2)	300	
Increase in working capital	(2 300)	
		(2 700)
NET OPERATING OUTFLOW		(1 300)
FINANCED BY		
Proceeds of share issue	1 050	
Long-term loan repayment	(500)	
Deterioration of liquid position (Note 1)	750	
		1 300

Notes: 1 The liquid position has changed by realisation of short-term investments £700, increase of cash in hand (£50) and increase in overdraft £100.
2 Profit before tax includes £50 profit on sale of fixed assets. The cash proceeds of these disposals were £300 + £50 = £350.

FIGURE 3:2 SOURCE AND APPLICATIONS OF FUNDS

3 Forecast gross capital expenditure on fixed assets
4 Calculate the depreciation provision
5 Appraise the proceeds of disposals of fixed assets
  Estimate the change in working capital

This gives the operating changes in the employment of funds. Then look at the financing side of the picture and find that:

7 There is a loan maturity to pay of £500
8 That leaves a deficit of £1800, of which £700 is to come from realising short-term investments, and the rest from a share issue and minor changes in the cash and overdraft positions which will leave the company within its negotiated overdraft facility of £1600.

The procedure for carrying out these tasks is as follows:

The *profit* is estimated by looking at the budget and perhaps deducting something for the normal tendency to underachieve it.

Tax and dividend payments can usually be assessed quite accurately from facts known at the beginning of the year. In the case of tax, provisions are checked against the progress of negotiations with the Inspector.

Capital expenditure, depreciation and *fixed assets disposals* are also likely to give little trouble, as long as it is remembered that capital expenditure budgets are usually considerably in excess of actual expenditure. In forecasting, however, fixed assets disposals should normally be taken at the cash proceeds level (£350 rather than £300 in Figure 3:2) and exclude the profit on disposal of fixed assets: this makes the profit in that example £3450 instead of £3500.

Forecasting working capital

This is the really difficult task. The first point to note is that the order of approach is reversed. In all the above cases—capital expenditure, depreciation, profit—the events of the year are assessed first, before arriving at the balance sheet items at the end of the year. In the case of working capital we have to arrive at the balance sheet item before we work out the change for the year (by comparing the balance sheet item at the beginning and end).

The second point is that in order to forecast working capital, either as a single figure or in detail, for as long ahead as twelve months, we have to know the *level of activity* at that future point of time.

In other words, if detailed working capital budgets (which are recommended in chapter 2 and elsewhere in this book) are not available, but a forecast of the likely cash position twelve months from now is nonetheless required, then at least something must be known about the level of activity, and the most readily available figure is the sales turnover. If it is known that last year there was a turnover of £20 000 and a working capital at the end of the year of 30% = £6000, and if this year the forecast turnover is £29 000, then at first sight it would be reasonable to put the year-end working capital at 30% of £29 000 = £8700. However, we happen to know that last year there was an abnormal stock of one component which is being run down this year, so that a more normal ratio is 28.6% which gives a forecast of £8300.

This is a much oversimplified approach. Working capital should be controlled and therefore forecast in greater detail, and none of the elements are directly related to the previous twelve months' sales. For example, finished stocks should perhaps be related to the *subsequent one* month's *cost* of sales; but all these matters are more fully dealt with in Chapter 2 and elsewhere in this book. The fact remains that if sales are rising on a reasonably steady trend, then working capital is likely to change roughly in proportion to sales, unless efficiency changes, and a change in efficiency is tantamount to a change in the ratio of working capital to turnover.

Liquidity statements and cash forecasts

A source and application of funds statement can be presented in such a way that it begins and ends with the net liquid position. It is then called a liquidity statement. Figure 3:2 could be restated as a liquidity forecast as in Figure 3:3.

This presentation still belongs to the family of source and applications of funds statements, whose members have the common characteristic that they are cast broadly in accounting terms. They invariably include profit, depreciation, and changes in fixed assets and working capital.

There is, however, an alternative way of presenting or summarising the change from the opening to the closing liquid position. This follows the general line of a receipts and payments account, and looks at cash movements from the cashier's rather than the accountant's point of view.

The same year's events could then be forecast in the form shown in Figure 3:4.

The form of presentation used in Figure 3:4 is called a "cash forecast". There are differences of opinion about the relative merits of cash forecasts and liquidity forecasts of the source and applications variety. One is the cashier's and the other the accountant's view of the same facts.

	£
Liquid position at 1 January	(1 400)
Pre-tax profit £3450 less payments	
of tax £1500 and dividend £500	1 350
Capital expenditure (£1500) less depreciation (£800)	
and proceeds of disposal of fixed assets (£350)	(350)
Increase in working capital	(2 300)
Proceeds of share issue	1 050
Long-term loan repayment	(500)
Liquid position at 31 December	(2 150)

FIGURE 3:3 LIQUIDITY FORECAST

	£	£
Overdraft balance at 1 January		(1 400)
RECEIPTS		
Collections from customers	28 750	
Cash from share issue	1 050	
Proceeds of disposals of fixed assets	350	
		30 150
PAYMENTS		
For purchases	18 500	
Wages, salaries	5 750	
For fixed assets	1 550	
For expenses	2 500	
Tax	1 600	
Dividend	500	
Long-term debt instalment	500	
		(30900)
Overdraft balance at 31 December		(2 150)

1 *Notes:* For the sake of simplicity it is assumed that the net liquid position is made up of just the overdraft balance.

2 Collections from customers are not exactly equal to sales, which are £29 000; nor are payments for fixed assets equal to capital expenditure of £1 500. The differences represent changes in debtors and creditors.

FIGURE 3:4 CASH FORECAST

Frequency and period covered by forecasts

Cash forecasts are generally more reliable over periods of up to a month, and liquidity forecasts for long periods of a year or more. This is because at the end of that period, account must be taken of the expected level of activity at that time. In any case the cashier's method could extrapolate receipts and payments in such a way as to imply absurdities like negative inventories at the end of a longer period.

Most businesses need to assess and update the cash outlook monthly for the next three months and quarterly for the next four quarters. Once a year they should also look five years ahead, so as to plan cash resources and warn management in time against overtrading.

It follows that the near-middle distance, two to eleven months ahead, is one that has to be appraised at regular intervals. The sensible thing to do is to cast all projections in source and applications of funds form, but to check the earlier period against a receipts and payments type of forecast prepared by the cashier's method.

4

Sources and Use of Long-term Finance

Equity and reserves

Equity is an alternative name for the shareholders' capital which includes their shares and the reserves. It increases automatically in response to the net profit or decreases in response to net loss but this does not change the shareholders' position relative to one another.

For example, four shareholders owning one quarter of the shares each will all become £100 richer when a profit of £400 is made, by the rise in value of their shares; but they all still stand equal to one another in voting power and in entitlement to future dividends.

When new shares are issued as a bonus to the existing shareholders the effect is to reduce the reserves by the same amount as the shares are increased. No extra cash comes into the company so the shareholders still have the same position relative to one another and there has been no alteration to the working capital.

When new shares are issued for cash the effect is very different. Net current assets will increase because cash is one of the elements although if new fixed assets are being bought they may very soon cause a transfer away from the working capital to the fixed assets. The real problem is that voting power and the position of shareholders relative to one another will change unless all the existing shareholders subscribe equal amounts and if no outsiders subscribe.

Introducing new shareholders

New shareholders coming into the company on equal footing with existing shareholders are taking over a part of the valuable but intan-

BEFORE NEW ISSUE		AFTER NEW ISSUE		
Shares £1 each	100			200
Reserves	40	Original	40	
	——	Share premium		
		reserve	140	180
	140		——	——
				380
Loans	60			60
	——			——
	200			440
	——			——
Fixed assets	120			120
Net current assets (current		Original	80	
assets, including cash		Add cash from		
less current		new shares	100	
liabilities)	80	and premium	140	320
	——		——	——
	200			440
	——			——

Note 1

Estimated value of goodwill				
not disclosed in balance				
sheet	100			100
	——			——
This goodwill is owned by				
(*a*) the original shareholders				
—whole	100	(*a*)		50
(*b*) the new shareholders	—	(*b*)		50
	——			——
	100			100
	——			——

Note 2

Value of shares is as			
shown in balance sheet	£140	As in balance sheet	380
plus goodwill	£100	plus goodwill	100
	——		——
	£240		£480
	——		——
Each share is worth	£2.40		£2.40

FIGURE 4:1 ISSUE OF NEW SHARES AT A PREMIUM

gible asset known as goodwill. To take this into account and to recompense the existing shareholders for what they have given up it is customary to demand a premium payment on the new shares. This premium is added to the capital reserves of the company and serves to balance out the rights of the new and existing shareholders equitably.

Figure 4:1 illustrates the way net current assets are increased by bringing in new cash from additional shareholders including the amount they pay for the share premium. The correct sequence of events is:

1 The directors work out how much additional funds they need to cover any planned expansion of both working capital and fixed assets.
2 They estimate the value of the goodwill, this being a question of judging how much potential investors will be willing to pay rather than applying some arbitrary formula. The formulas used for calculating goodwill are a rough guide to its worth but not a positive statement.
3 Work the forecast balance sheet "backwards," that is:
(*a*) Complete the assets side at the desired level.
(*b*) Split the figure of total extra cash between new shares and premium in such a proportion that the value of each share both old and new would be the same as the value of the original share, including the goodwill prior to the new issue.

Long-term loans for smaller companies

In order to raise a long-term loan a company must have solid security to offer. The prospect of earning regular profits sufficient to meet the interest is also important and without it there would be little chance of an application for a loan being successful, but profitability by itself would not suffice without the backing of the security.

These pre-conditions effectively restrict the occasions for raising long-term loans (other than the renewals of the old ones which have just fallen due for repayment) to the times when new land or buildings are being bought. Of course, those few companies which have not yet borrowed against their existing premises always have the opportunity before them.

The sources which these companies may try for their loans are:

1 ICFC (Industrial and Commercial Finance Corporation Ltd). This organisation lends mainly to industrial companies seeking amounts between £5000 and £250 000. The Corporation places much more emphasis on the client's profitability than on the value of the security.

This means that although they will seldom dispense with security entirely there is a chance of obtaining a loan which bears a very satisfactory ratio to the value of the security being offered. Repayment period may be arranged between five and twenty-five years and terms are fairly flexible.

2 *Insurance companies.* Most of the large insurance companies will consider this type of business, but the security in land and buildings is essential. Repayment may be arranged to suit individual requirements, and very long periods such as thirty to forty years are popular with some of the insurance companies. Many of them are happier with loans over £100 000 than with the amounts more appropriate to the numerous smaller companies.

3 *Pension funds.* Various pension funds advertise their willingness to advance funds against the security of industrial or commercial premises. Some of them have a preference for the sale and lease-back system which serves the same purpose of providing the industrial company with immediate funds but transfers the present prospect of capital growth in the value of the premises to their new owners.

Long-term loans for large companies

Public companies may obtain loans from insurance companies or pension funds against suitable security just as the smaller firms and probably on more favourable terms.

In addition, they may invite the public to subscribe for unsecured loan stock dated for repayment in a period ranging from two to thirty years. Interest rates tend to be high and even the largest international companies have been offering ten to eleven per cent per annum on issues during 1970.

Retained profit as a source of working capital

Profit increases working capital, and is one of the most satisfactory sources of liquid funds. Directors deciding the company's dividend policy must keep in mind that the dividend itself will abstract a portion of the year's profit, whilst leaving the remainder as a permanent or semipermanent addition to the working capital.

The place of profit in provision of liquid funds is illustrated in Figure 4:2.

	EXAMPLE £'000
Sales = cash ± variation in debtors	
Main source of incoming cash is from sales	100
Offset by payment of expenses & interest	(70)
	───
Balance = depreciation + profit	30
Deduct depreciation (an amount depending	
on personal judgement)	(10)
	───
Balance = profit	20
deduct corporation tax	(8)
	───
Profit available for distribution	12
deduct dividend payment	(7)
	───
Balance = retained profit = permanent/semi-	
permanent addition to liquid resources	5
	───

FIGURE 4:2   PLACE OF PROFIT IN THE AVAILABLE FUNDS

The retained profit, being cash, is an addition to net current assets. It is even an addition to working capital whilst still remaining in the form of extra trade debtors. The addition is permanent until such time as a decision is reached to withdraw further amounts as dividend, or until it is offset by further spending on fixed assets or working capital.

The proposed dividend is a temporary addition to net current assets for the interval between earning the profit and paying the dividend. This interval may be extended at the discretion of the directors, by delaying the annual general meeting and the declaration of the dividend.

Dividends should not be delayed beyond the end of the fiscal year, 5 April, as this could leave shareholders with a year with no income and the following year having double income heavily hit by surtax.

Most companies consider it preferable to hold their AGM and declare their dividends during the same month each year.

A dividend declared at the start of a taxation month (at present the sixth day of the month) will take six weeks credit before the due date for handing to the Revenue the tax deducted from the dividends. To declare the dividend later in the tax month is to enjoy a shorter period of credit.

Each year's addition to the company's general reserves by way of this retained profit increases also the shareholders' total investment in their company. They may reasonably expect to see higher profits in future years, and the directors should appreciate that the profit does not "belong to the company"; it belongs to the shareholders. If they had taken it out in the shape of larger dividend then they could have re-invested it elsewhere to give them a return of X per cent per annum. By leaving it in the company under the control of the directors they should obtain an increased return at least equal to X per cent, and preferably to $X + Y$ per cent because their own directors, using risk capital, should produce better returns than are shown by gilt-edged securities.

	£	£
Original investment, 1 January 1970		100 000
Profit for year to		
31 December 1970. 25%	25 000	
Less corporation tax	10 000	
	15 000	
Less dividend	5 000	
Balance added to reserves	10 000	10 000
Shareholders' investment in the company at		
1 January 1971		110 000
Profit for year to		
31 December 1971.		
Same 25% but on £110 000	27 500	
Less corporation tax	11 000	
	16 500	
Dividend	5 500	
Balance added to reserves	11 000	11 000
Shareholders' investment in the company at 1 January 1972		121 000

FIGURE 4:3   RETURN ON AN INCREASING SHAREHOLDERS' INVESTMENT

In Figure 4:3, the company's pre-tax profit for 1971 had been less than £27 500, the company's efficiency in creating profits would have been below the 1970 standard.

For the year 1972 the required profit to keep up the same standard will be 25% of £121 000 = £30 250.

5

Sources and Use of Short-term Finance

This chapter examines various aspects of short-term finance from the point of view of a manufacturing company. Generally, attention is concentrated on financing operations in the UK.

Before considering various sources of finance, a close look should be taken at the business, to analyse critically just what it is that is being financed, why the money is needed and for how long, and why the search is for short-term money. The difference between correct and incorrect financing can make a difference to profitability, and most mistakes are made in identifying the problem rather than in selecting the right source of money. Before looking in the shop window, the company should submit to a thorough examination to make sure that it has identified the exact requirements.

1 *Why not raise equity?* Is profitability and market rating too low to permit a rights issue on acceptable terms? Or could earnings per share be improved by additional gearing?

2 *Why not borrow long?* Is it for market reasons? Is the company bumping against the limits of the debentures trust deed? Or are present needs too small or too temporary to warrant a long-term funding operation?

3 *Is this the sort of company that finances its business generally or contract by contract?* Plant engineers and large civil engineering contractors, for example, are at any one time engaged in only a handful of large contracts, and their cash requirements depend entirely on how many such contracts they have in hand. Such companies will normally arrange finance for each contract. Most other businesses will plan their resources for the business as a whole for periods of (say) a year at a time.

4 *Is the finance required for fixed assets, raw materials, work-in-progress, finished stocks or debtors?*

5 *During the period for which cash resources are being planned are there any major receipts or payments and on what dates?* Examples are tax payments, dividend payments, loan maturities or instalments, acquisitions for cash, or dividends from major investments.

6 *What is the company's reputation with suppliers, bankers and other lenders?* This obviously influences the number of options which are open to the company.

Traditionally, short-term finance has been concerned with current rather than fixed assets. However, this is not logical because many fixed assets diminish in value through their working lives, thus cutting down the need for funds year by year, whereas current assets represent a stream of successive stocks and debtors, a large part of which is likely to be permanently required in a continuing business.

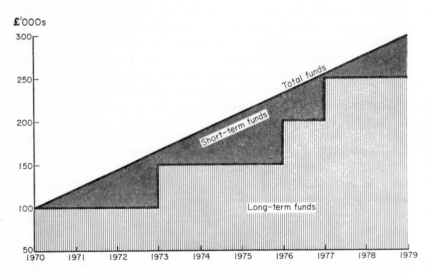

FIGURE 5:1   THE CONSTANT LEAPFROG OF LONG-
AND SHORT-TERM FINANCE

Short-term finance should be used:

1 To meet the difference between peak and minimum working capital requirements in a seasonal trade.

2 To meet the fluctuation within each month in a trade where payments are spread evenly through the month but receipts are bunched at the end of the month.

3 To meet the demand for extra funds caused by expansion of the trade, until such time as the expansion is recognised to be permanent. In most growing companies there will be a leapfrogging effect with long-term funds being raised every three to five years and short-term borrowing covering the growth between these steps. Figure 5:1 illustrates this principle.

Alternative sources of short-term finance

The various short-term facilities are discussed partly in this chapter, partly in Chapter 12; the ECGD-backed facilities are discussed in Chapter 14.

It is useful to classify possible sources according to their effect on the balance sheet. This is useful, firstly, because it is always a good idea to think in terms of future planned balance sheets and, secondly, because not everyone remembers those facilities which can be tapped by reducing the ownership of assets.

The opportunity to factor the trade debtors should be included amongst the possibilities. The classification is then as follows (including certain topics discussed in other chapters).

1 *Finance which reduces assets instead of creating liabilities.* This includes, for example, buying stocks on consignment, factoring debtors, or raising non-recourse finance for exports under one of the schemes backed by the Export Credits Guarantee Department (ECGD) (see Chapter 14).

2 *Finance which reduces assets and appears as a contingent liability.* This includes for example customers' trade bills discounted.

3 *Finance which appears as borrowings.* This includes loans and overdrafts from clearing banks, or from other banks and lenders, acceptance credits, a variety of foreign-currency borrowings and with-recourse export finance.

4 *Other credits shown as liabilities.* This includes liabilities for corporation tax, SET or VAT, PAYE, National Insurance contributions, holiday pay and the like, as well as trade credit from suppliers.

Basic principles in selecting sources

It is assumed that the company has as one of its chief objectives the satisfaction of its shareholders by maximising its share price. Consequently, the company will be interested above all in maximising its earnings per share.

In selecting sources of short-term funds the company will go for the following tactical objectives, some of which are likely to conflict with one another:

1   Cheapness, e.g. minimum rate of interest
2   Flexibility, to give room for future manoeuvre in such events as (i) unexpected shortages or extra requirements and (ii) changes in the interest rate structure
3   Avoidance of risks
4   Bridging the correct time-gap, e.g. until funding or until the next seasonal inflow of funds

In any cost comparisons it is, of course, the *opportunity* cost that must be compared. Suppose, for example, that the overdraft facility at $8\frac{1}{2}\%$ is already being used to the hilt, and that to meet an extra requirement there are only two choices available: to forfeit a $2\frac{1}{2}\%$ cash discount allowed by a major supplier or to lease, instead of buy, an item of capital equipment. Let us assume that the effective cost of leasing is $12\frac{1}{2}\%$ a year, and that the supplier's invoice will fall due for payment after ninety days unless payment is made within seven days to collect the discount. The effective cost of forfeiting the discount in that case is $2\frac{1}{2}\% \times \dfrac{365 \text{ days}}{90\text{--}7 \text{ days}} = 11\%$. Clearly, therefore, it is better to forfeit the discount. If unused overdraft facility had been available, the opportunity cost would be $8\frac{1}{2}\%$; as there is not, the opportunity cost is $12\frac{1}{2}\%$ and it clearly pays to incur the extra effective cost of 11%.

Examples of conflict between the tactical objectives are:

1   In many situations overdrafts are the cheapest source of cash. They are also the most convenient and most readily mobilised source, and to use the facility to the hilt is to sacrifice the margin for unexpected contingencies. In other words, cheapness conflicts with flexibility.

2   Suppose it is possible to borrow sterling at $8\frac{1}{2}\%$, but D-marks could be borrowed at 6%. The funds are needed by a German subsidiary. Either the subsidiary can borrow locally or the parent company can give it 90 days' credit instead of 30 and borrow in the UK. As the D-marks have to be repaid in that currency there is a risk of an exchange loss. Cheapness conflicts with the desire to avoid risks. Now suppose that the D-marks can be covered forward at a cost of less than $2\frac{1}{2}\%$, say at 2% a year. Then it clearly pays to borrow the D-marks after all, as the funds can be obtained at an effective certain cost of 8%, $\frac{1}{2}\%$ less than the cost of borrowing sterling. In this last case we have been able to escape the conflict by paying a profitable insurance premium to eliminate the risk.

3 Sometimes the conflict is between short-term and long-term profits as when it is possible immediately to obtain a 360-day loan at $\frac{1}{2}\%$ below the overdraft rate, but there is good reason to expect a drop of at least 1% in the overdraft rate within the next two to three months. If there are adequate margins within the overdraft limit, it would probably be best to decline the 360-day loan.

Trade credit

Whenever governments restrict credit or liquidity, the subject of trade credit receives greater attention. In the 1950s some economists believed that in a squeeze the big companies found themselves financing smaller ones; by now it is more commonly believed that the reverse happens. However, these generalisations oversimplify the problem and ignore the great variety of situations within this field.

The point about trade credit is that it is simply one aspect of the complex relationship between buyer and seller. What persuades them to do business with each other is the relative attractiveness of the entire package of price, delivery, quality, technical excellence, reputation, reliability, and credit terms. Credit terms are sometimes unimportant within this package, and sometimes rather more important, depending on how illiquid the customer is and how much of a financing problem a particular purchase is. It can also depend on the extent to which, say, buyers are in touch with, or even aware of, their company's financial position and policies.

Generally, it is probably desirable that trade credit should not play an excessive part in the buying decision. If there is a good supplier, there is a corresponding vested interest in his financial health and happiness, and it might not be in the company's interest to press him too hard for more credit.

Finally, there is the question whether it is profitable to pay promptly for the sake of a cash discount. This needs to be calculated carefully on the opportunity cost principle. The first step is to identify the span of time between the date on which we have to pay to collect the discount and the date on which we should otherwise pay. Let us say that the dates are day 7 and day 98 after delivery respectively, so that the gap is 91 days or $\frac{1}{4}$ of a year. In that case a $2\frac{1}{2}\%$ cash discount represents an interest rate of $4 \times 2\frac{1}{2}\% = 10\%$. Therefore if the alternative source of money available costs less than 10%, then it is more profitable to take the discount. But if the time-gap had been 114 days, so that the discount would have represented a rate of interest of only 8%, whereas the overdraft costs (say) $8\frac{1}{2}\%$, then it would have been more advantageous to go without the discount, as in this case the overdraft is the dearer source of cash. On the other hand, if there is no margin of unused overdraft facility left, and if marginal alternative funds cost 11%, then it would be cheaper to go without the discount as long as the time gap is more than 83 days, as $2\frac{1}{2}\% \times \dfrac{365}{83} = 11\%$.

Bank overdrafts

In September 1971, the long-established system of tying the interest rate on overdrafts to Bank Rate was changed. Interest rates are now geared to Base Rate, which can vary from one clearing bank to another. Nevertheless an overdraft is still usually the cheapest and always the most flexible and convenient source of short-term finance. The convenience is in its instant availability plus the fact that interest is payable on outstanding balances only. The comparative inconvenience of a bank loan is that during its term it carries interest irrespective of whether the borrower has a useful employment for the whole amount or has some of it idle as a credit balance on current account.

In a well-conducted company the object of cash management should be to have a cushion against unexpected and peak requirements, and the best form in which to hold this cushion is a tranche of unused overdraft facility.

Each company has to determine what cushion it needs in the light of its business. A useful guide might be one or two per cent of its annual turnover, representing about one half to one week's collections. In some businesses, seasonal fluctuations in weekly collections need to be taken into account.

Suppose there are annual collections of £5.2 million—that is, £100 000 a week—so that our cushion should be anything up to that figure of £100 000. Suppose also that we cannot negotiate a larger overdraft limit than £1 million, and our cash forecast shows requirements of £2 million. In that case we should be well advised to allow for a cushion of at least £100 000 and to arrange finance from some source other than overdrafts of at least £1.1 million, so that only a maximum of £900 000 of our requirements is planned to come out of the overdraft facility.

A company using bank overdraft facilities must, of course, exercise proper control over this type of short-term finance. Figure 5:2 charts the effects of three different management approaches to the use of a bank overdraft.

In this example, the company has arranged for a bank overdraft to a maximum of £20 000 and the bank manager expects to see a fluctuating balance with an occasional approach to zero.

The trade is seasonal, and within each month receipts are bunched to give the most favourable balance to the company about the middle of the month.

Other sources of finance should be arranged so that the overdraft is patterned along the line *AA*. This meets zero at one point. At no time does it touch the agreed limit. Only once does it pass the reserve line at £16 000 which the directors had regarded as leaving a desirable margin of £4 000 to meet unforeseen eventualities.

Whether this reserve is large enough or too large must depend on individual circumstances in the company and past experience will have shown the extent to which the unexpected can hit the company's finances.

The line *BB* shows the position where the company is relying much too heavily on the bank. Through most of the year they are below the £16 000 reserve line. From May to September they are shown as exceeding the agreed limit of the overdraft. This is extremely dangerous. The bank are under no obligation to permit this unauthorised extension and the company could find the facility completely withdrawn at short notice.

Where the forecast shows the line to be similar to *BB*, immediate steps should be taken. These could be either to raise extra funds from other sources or to cut down the need for funds by modifying the plans for the year.

Line *CC* is ultra-safe. It shows the same pattern of rise and fall in the bank balance but it starts and continues with a substantial balance in hand instead of being overdrawn. The overdraft facility is not being used at all and the resources of working capital have drifted into an idle balance on the current account. This company should check its plans against Appendix 1 dealing with the reversal of the normal plan of management of working capital.

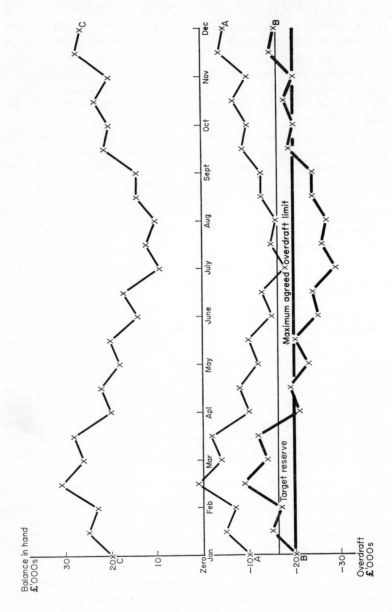

FIGURE 5:2   MANAGEMENT CONTROL OF
BANK OVERDRAFT

Inter-company loans

Another source which is becoming popular is the inter-company market. We have seen that governmental restrictions can have an effect on the pattern of trade credit, but the possibilities are obviously not limited to credit between companies which happen to be selling to one another. Contact is usually through banks, merchant banks or stock-brokers, and rates are obviously a matter for negotiation. Lenders may well need some security, as the very existence of this market is due to tight money conditions.

Conclusions

From the matters reviewed in this chapter, the following general conclusions may be drawn:

1   Before raising short-term funds from any source it is worth identifying objectives and needs
2   The criteria for selecting between sources are opportunity cost, flexibility, risk and length of time
3   There are more sources than it is sometimes realised, especially for financing exports, and it is worth watching for new sources
4   Some forms of borrowing need a fair amount of expertise to manage, and all of them must be planned

Part Three
Financial Control of Trade Debtors

6

Establishing a Policy for Trade Debtors

For any trading concern selling goods or services on credit, debtors must be regarded as a permanent feature of working capital. They invariably represent expensive funds tied up, but properly and carefully managed, they can, and should, make a positive contribution to increased turnover and profits.

As debtors settle their accounts, cash flows into the company but at the same time new sales produce new debts and thus the level of trade debtors remains more or less constant (given the same volume of turnover).

Management policies with regard to trade debtors vary from company to company, depending on a number of factors such as the nature of the company's sales (seasonal, cyclical, expanding), characteristics of the company's market and its general credit policies.

Some companies follow a deliberate policy of granting liberal credit terms in order to increase their turnover and encourage those customers who would otherwise be unable or reluctant to buy the company's goods.

The degree of risk involved in selling goods on credit is recognised by every well-managed company in the special provision for bad debts, which is normally set off against the amount due from trade debtors. Since the collapse of Rolls-Royce, followed by a number of bankruptcies, the danger of even the best blue-chip customer becoming insolvent has increased, emphasising the need for stricter control of trade debtors.

A norm for the risk, however, may be established with reasonable accuracy and the larger the spread over different customers, the more reliable the norm will be.

The company's credit controller sets his standard according to his interpretation of references, status reports and any other information regarding the circumstances of the company's potential customers.

In assessing the cost of debtors as a non-productive asset in the company's operations, the management must decide whether by reducing the average level of debtors it could also cut the cost of its most expensive source of borrowed funds. Figure 6:1 illustrates this problem.

1971		1972	
Sales	£120 000	Sales	£120 000
Average level of debtors	30 000	Reduced level of debtors	20 000
Funds borrowed	£15 000	Funds borrowed	£5 000
Interest at 12% a year	£1 800	Interest	£600
		Saving	£1 200

FIGURE 6:1   CUTTING INTEREST COSTS BY
REDUCING DEBTORS

This reduction is equivalent to an improvement of 0.8 per cent on the net profit, which is a very considerable amount for companies whose net profit rarely exceeds 8 or 9 per cent.

In some cases, an increase in debtors may be justified in spite of the heavy cost involved in borrowing additional funds if it can be shown that by offering extended credit facilities the volume of sales has been increased, thus producing a larger net profit. This course of action is acceptable only if the extra profit earned on higher turnover exceeds the cost of obtaining additional funds.

Figure 6:2 describes a situation in which an increased turnover resulting from easier credit terms has failed to improve net profit because of the high cost of financing a larger volume of debtors.

The extension of credit and increase in trade debtors will inevitably increase the amount of capital employed and generate the need for funds to finance it.

If the company is unable to raise extra capital from normal sources it may be forced to postpone payments to creditors, thus increasing its current liabilities.

	1971		1972
Sales	£120 000		£180 000
Average level of debtors (3-month settlement)	30 000	(4-month settlement)	60 000
Average net profit before interest payable on additional funds	£6 000		£9 000
Cost of funds borrowed (10% on £30 000)	(3 000)	(10% on £60 000)	(6 000)
Net profit after deducting interest on loan	£3 000		£3 000

FIGURE 6:2   RAISING TURNOVER BY ALLOWING LONGER CREDIT

This increase may be offset by a similar increase in debtors and the total amount of working capital will remain unchanged. If the creditors, however, are unwilling to extend the settlement period and are pressing for payment, the company may find itself in a dangerous situation.

Factoring the debts

One effective and permanent way to turn the asset "trade debtors" into cash is to sell them to a debt factor. Several companies have been established in the UK as debt factors during the 1960s and their trade has been expanding rapidly as the advantages have been more widely appreciated.

Details of the system vary slightly from one company to another, but the main pattern of their activities is set out below. One of the more important differences is the question whether the factor carries the risk and burden of bad debts or whether the client must reimburse him for them.

When the factor does meet the bad debts his charges must be higher, the difference being roughly in line with the cost of premiums for insuring against bad debts and standing in their place. Also he will reserve the right to dictate to the client about credit limits for established customers and the approval of new customers on the basis of trade references and other credit risk enquiries.

This means the factoring of debts is neither a licence to start trading with all the shaky firms who are willing to buy, nor a cheap way of escaping the consequences of weak credit control. Its function is primarily to release working capital for other purposes, and this it does very effectively though rather expensively.

The effect of factoring on the working capital is illustrated in Figure 6:3.

The company is carrying a wider range of stock after starting the factoring operation. This stock has been carefully chosen for its contribution to attracting and satisfying more customers. There are no longer any overdue accounts with dissatisfied creditors, and the firm has spare funds in the bank to use for still more trading.

Note particularly that the growth in sales is not the result of the factoring. It is the result of increased sales effort on the part of the company's staff and management. The place of the factoring in the transaction has been to enable the company to finance its higher working capital which inevitably accompanies a rise in sales turnover.

Routine of factoring

When an agreement for factoring has been made, sales invoices are issued daily or weekly to the factors who attend to all bookkeeping and collecting of debts. This makes a useful economy of administrative costs for the trading company.

At the end of each week the factors send their client a cheque equal to the week's sales invoices, so that trade debtors regularly vary between zero and a single week's sales, instead of two to four months' sales.

The cost of the service is a percentage of the average amount owed to the trader. The rate depends on the nature of the trader's business and on the factoring company. It is fair to say that some factors have higher charges than others, and some are prepared to negotiate their terms whilst others are rigidly fixed.

For a company whose customers pay on average within six weeks, the cost of factoring will be only about half that for a firm whose customers take twelve weeks to settle.

A few factor companies are willing to take on clients for short periods and to take only a proportion of their credit accounts, but the majority insist on a long-term contract and on the whole of the credit sales being within the contract.

1. The working capital section of the balance sheet:

	Before factoring	After factoring
	£'00	£'00
Stock	10 000	12 000
Debtors	8 000	0
Cash	0	1 000
Total current assets	18 000	13 000
less creditors (many overdue for settlement)	9 000 (all up to date)	4 000
Net current assets	9 000	9 000

N.B. The total is not changed by the factoring operation, but the content of the net current assets is drastically altered.

2. The corresponding change in the pattern of trading:

	Year prior to factoring	Year following start of factoring
	£'00	£'00
Sales turnover	60 000	90 000
Gross profit on trading 30%	18 000	30% 27 000
Fixed overheads	12 000	14 000*
		13 000
	Factoring charges	2 250
Net profit, 6% of sales	6 000	10 750

FIGURE 6:3   EFFECT OF FACTORING THE TRADE DEBTS

Gross improvement due to factoring—sales and gross profit both increased by 50 per cent.

Net improvement due to factoring £10 750 − £6 000 = £4 750

* Fixed overheads are never truly fixed, so they have been shown as increasing slightly but not proportionately to the growth in sales. The factoring charges have been taken as 10% of average outstanding debts equal to three months' sales, £22 500. This is merely an illustration and actual charges depend on circumstances peculiar to each company.

Most factors are interested only in clients whose turnover is above £100 000, but in exceptional circumstances some will take on companies with a smaller turnover, particularly where there are prospects of rapid growth.

Conclusions

For a company which is expanding rapidly with profitable trade, and so almost inevitably is short of working capital, factoring the debts may be an ideal solution to its financial problems. The supply of funds from the factors expands in direct response to the growth of turnover, and the dangers of overtrading are almost completely cut out.

Against this it will be found that the costs are higher than for interest on bank overdraft, or on secured loans, such as might be used to finance the trade debtors. Therefore, factoring will rarely be used by companies which are able to borrow enough funds to meet their trading requirements. Nor will they be used where profit margins are too low to carry the factor's charges and still leave a good margin of net profit for the shareholders.

In a company with a relatively large proportion of fixed costs compared to variable costs, extra sales tend to be doubly profitable because the whole of the difference between selling price and variable costs is profit once the main sales have covered the fixed costs. Therefore, the marginal costing approach described in Chapter 7 will be used to help in a decision whether to use expensive factoring as part of a programme for expanding sales.

7

Management of Trade Debtors

Role of credit controller

Except for companies which sell only on a cash basis, credit sales
generate trade debtors with the consequent need to finance, out of
working capital, the interval between the date of sale and the date of
payment. The amount of capital so employed represents an investment
by the seller in the buyer. The seller will therefore find it prudent to
check and control the soundness of his investment and to investigate
the cost of utilising working capital for this purpose.

The function of working capital and the analysis of cash flow including the receivable element has been dealt with in Chapter 6 from which
it will be seen that the amount of capital employed in this area is gov-
erned by two factors, sales volume and time delay. This chapter will
examine how the credit controller takes account of these factors and
of the *quality* of the debt—that is, how risky it is.

The marketing/sales team will generate debtors but will not, as a
rule, give serious initial consideration to the quality of the debt as an
asset once their operation has converted it into a debt from stock. It
is in this respect that the closest liaison and understanding is essential
between the sales and the credit departments. This liaison is best
achieved by the company having a formal credit policy worked out
and accepted by both sales and credit managements. The policy should
set out quite clearly that far from their being a conflict of interests, as
is usually thought to be the case, the interests of both sectors of the
business are identical. This can be broadly stated as "to maximise
sales and profits with the minimum of risk." The policy should show
quite clearly who is responsible for the credit function. It may be the

company accountant, secretary, or even sales manager, but in the larger companies it will be economical to employ a properly trained credit controller who will concentrate his whole attention on this subject. It should be recognised that credit cannot be delegated to a junior employee because it is easy for an unskilled person to upset a customer and because customers simply ignore applications from staff whose requests lack the ring of authority. The place of junior staff is to keep the records up to date and feed the information to the credit controller who will take action on it. The credit controller's role is to extend such credit as is necessary for the success of the company's sales effort.

"Extending credit" implies a positive approach rather than the negative "restricting credit." Given this positive policy with its proper application, the sales department will come to consult the credit manager once it understands that his role is that of counsellor as well as debt collector, that his job is to pave the financial path to a successful financial outcome to each transaction. They will accept the simple fact that it is of no use to allow a first-class selling job to convert perfectly good stock into a thoroughly bad debt. They will also come to understand that the profit is made only after the customer has paid for the material or service. On the other hand credit management must actively accept the fact that it is sales which generate earnings and keep this basic fact to the fore when operating the credit function.

If at all possible, the credit policy should leave no doubt as to who is finally responsible for fixing payment terms and conditions. This must be a matter for individual company policy. It should be remembered however that providing he has a real awareness of his responsibility to sales, it is or should be the credit manager who is the expert in this function of the investment of working capital in debtors so that the final decision should be his.

Trade debtors or receivables constitute one of the main liquid assets of the average company and therefore a proper control is essential at all times. It is a maxim that "the longer the credit the bigger the risk"; in other words, the longer the debt is outstanding the harder it becomes to collect. The objectives of credit management must be then to have the highest possible volume of outstanding debt for the shortest possible time commensurate with increasing credit sales and the availability of funds to finance them.

It is obvious that the control and management of this important asset should be in the hands of someone fully qualified for the job with the time available to do it properly. Whether or not the credit control function shall be a part- or full-time job must of course depend upon the company, its sales volume and/or its number of accounts. The important thing is that the role should not be considered lightly nor left entirely in the hands of sales who by the very nature of their function will take an over-optimistic view of the outcome. The role of credit controller should be specifically designated, appointed and executed. The function is composed of two major sectors:

1   Risk assessment and fixing credit limits
2   Debt collection and ledger maintenance

In a very small company the one person responsible for actually posting the sales ledger is generally a bookkeeper and general clerk by nature and training, and is unsuited to the duties of a credit controller. Either the sales director or the managing director will probably need to undertake the credit control function personally in a business of this size.

Control of time delay

It has been traditional to measure the effectiveness of the control of trade debtors by making a comparison of trade debtors to turnover in months or days as in Figure 7:

£'000	Jan	Feb	Mar	Apr	May	June
Sales	100	110	90	120	125	110
Debtors				310	305	285

Then:
April debtors £310 000 = April sales, £120 000 plus March sales £90 000
plus 90% of February sales i.e. 2.90 months' sales
May debtors £305 000 = May sales £125 000 plus April sales £120 000
plus 66% March sales i.e. 2.66 months' sales
June debtors £285 000 = June sales £110 000 plus May sales £125 000
plus 50% April sales i.e. 2.50 months' sales

FIGURE 7:1   REDUCING AVERAGE LENGTH OF CREDIT

This simple calculation reflecting the variations on monthly turnover shows a definite trend of improvement in the amount of working capital tied up in debtors.

It is useful too to compare this figure not only month by month or quarter by quarter but also against a precalculated target figure. Perhaps the most usual of all payment terms is "30 days from the end of the month of dispatch." Because the first month is "free" a buyer who takes delivery on the 1st of a month will get a total of 60 days' credit whilst deliveries made on the 30th will involve only 30 days' credit. Thus the normal "30 days" does in fact mean straight away an average of 45 days' credit overall. If every customer therefore paid his account promptly on such terms, the target figure would be realistic at 1.5 months.

Some customers do not pay promptly and others need and are given longer terms and these variants from the basic 45 days must all be carefully investigated and added on. The extent of the addition must of course depend on traditional customs of the trade and the pattern of the business. It is also essential to take into account current economic conditions, the availability and price of money and so on. A governmental policy of restricting lending to damp down demand will be reflected in a shortage of cash at all levels of business and an increased taking of longer credit. In such conditions, with basic selling terms of "30" days it would not be unrealistic to set a debtors' target of 2.5 months of sales.

Figure 7:2 provides an example of over-investment in trade debtors as measured against a target of 2.5 months' delay.

April debtors 2.90 months Target 2.5 months Over-investment 0.4 months
May debtors 2.66 months Target 2.5 months Over-investment 0.16 months
June debtors 2.50 months Target 2.5 months Over-investment Nil
The over-investment of working capital in receivables can then be expressed in cash terms as:

April   £4 400 representing 0.4 of February sales
May   £1 440 representing 0.16 of March sales
June   Nil

FIGURE 7:2   OVER-INVESTMENT OF WORKING CAPITAL IN TRADE DEBTORS

It will be seen that although sales have fluctuated, there is over the three month April–June a marked reduction of the over-investment in debtors showing that collection performance is improving.

Another, more readily calculated formula is to divide debtors by sales and multiply by 365, the answer being the number of credit sales days outstanding. Thus:

$$\frac{\text{Receivables outstanding £120 000}}{\text{12 months' credit sales £500 000}} \times 365 = 87.6 \text{ credit sales days}$$

The important thing is to ensure that whatever formula is used, the trend is noted and, where necessary, rectifying measures taken at the earliest opportunity.

It should be noted that a continued downward trend in the average credit period is not of itself necessarily a good thing especially when it falls below the target figure. This could mean that the credit policy is being applied too stringently against the interests of sales. This is especially important if the downward trend in credit period is accompanied by a downward trend in sales.

An upward trend in credit period will require financing out of liquid resources and the attendant financing costs will reduce the profit margin unless proper provision has been made to cover such costs in the product price. A trade debt due from a customer of £5000 at a borrowing rate of 9 per cent costs £1.225 a day to finance. Accepting an order for £5000 at 90 days' credit makes the customer a present of about £112 unless the finance cost has been built into the price. In most cases debt services costs are calculated into the price to provide for the normal 30 days' credit period, or sometimes even for the average (target) credit period.

The client is given, or more usually, takes another two or three months and the additional cost of financing the working capital so tied up comes out of the profit margin. If our sale for £5000 is expected to show a profit of 5% assuming settlement in 30 days, another two months credit taken at 9% per annum costs £75 and will reduce that expected profit to only $3\frac{1}{2}\%$.

It will be seen therefore that there are three major elements in the management of receivables:

1 To extend such credit as is necessary for sales growth
2 To keep customers to the terms they have agreed
3 To refuse credit where there is reason to think the risk is unduly high

Credit assessment

Close liaison between credit management and sales department is essential to the success of both. It is the function of credit management not only to prevent sales from incurring bad debts or entering a business relationship that will give rise to expensive arrears but also to advise sales as to the strength and potential of a new client so that they can "go in" confidently and optimistically. For this reason a two-way feedback of information is essential for the development of good relations and mutual confidence.

The major questions to be answered in making any sort of credit sanction assessment can be broadly stated as:

1   Is the company operating anyway?
2   What is the history of its management?
3   What is the financial picture?
4   To what extent if any are the plant and premises owned or leased? What is their condition?
5   What are the company's growth plans—can they be financed, by whom?
6   What is the potential for our product with them?

Whatever the type of credit seeker is being assessed, these basic questions must be set down and answered. The answers are found by personal interview, commercial status reports, bank reports, representatives' field reports, personal or trade references, *The London Gazette*, etc.

For every client credit assessment there are two decisions to be made. How much and for how long? It is with these two questions in mind that the credit controller will analyse the information available to him.

"How much" relates, of course, to the credit limit, the amount of the account balance at any one time which the credit manager feels to be safely prudent as an investment by his company in the working capital of the debtor, the buyer. In order to maximise on selling possibilities, this credit limit should be set as high as possible in relation to the financial strength of the buyer and not necessarily geared to the currently normal monthly buying pattern.

"How long" concerns the length of time which the buyer wants or needs in terms of his own resources to pay. Generally speaking, the longer the credit period under negotiation, the higher the credit limit must be if sales potential is to be realised and finding the right balance between credit limit and credit period is perhaps the most difficult problem in credit assessment.

The commercial status report is obtainable from a number of reporting agencies, usually on a subscription basis. On payment, the subscriber is given a book or books of coupons which are completed and surrendered against a "coupon" tariff according to the nature and place of the enquiry. The commercial report varies widely in the nature of its content and the agency is very dependent upon the amount of information filed at Companies House. Under the Companies Act every limited company is required to file each year a copy of its accounts and its chairman's report. The Act, however, allows a company fifteen months after its financial year end to hold its annual general meeting at which the accounts are approved. As it is only after this meeting that the accounts are filed, they are in most cases already eighteen months out of date. Many companies are, however, even later in filing their annual return and, in fact, many do not bother to file any at all, and are therefore in breach of the law. However, assuming that the information is on file at Companies House in City Road, London EC1, the reporting agency will extract from it the names of the directors and their shareholding, the capital structure, relevant items from the balance sheet and accounts such as current assets, current liabilities, net worth, balance on the profit and loss account, details of debentures and charges outstanding and so on. The report will also, wherever possible, give some picture of the nature of the company's operations, its premises and the numbers on the payroll. It will also give as far as it can be obtained the credit and collection experience of other current suppliers, and will generally quote a credit amount which the agency regards as normal for the business.

The bank report can be obtained only if the name and branch of the client's bankers is known. Bank reports are seldom informative because, for obvious reasons, a bank cannot and will not speak ill of its own customer and will confine itself usually to an expression that the company is under capable management and is "considered good for the amount of the inquiry." The best bank report consists of one word, "Undoubted". Anything else given may be taken as a careful qualification of that banker's accolade.

Trade references are usually quoted by the credit seeker either voluntarily or on request. They are, of course, quite useful when read in conjunction with the other information available but the credit manager will check briefly on the quality of the referees given. It is not unknown for a credit seeker to quote a company or companies which have the same directors sitting on their respective boards and can therefore be relied on giving a first-class reference. One must watch also for the so-called "nursed account." It is not uncommon for a normally recalcitrant and slow payer to see to it that perhaps two or three of his bought ledger accounts, usually for small- or medium-sized figures are paid with unfailing regularity on due date. These are the companies that are always quoted as trade references and naturally they will speak very highly of their client. It is difficult to spot these nursed accounts but the warning lights should flash if the financial information obtained shows signs of poor liquidity and working capital shortage. In any event a new client is unlikely to quote as a reference a supplier with whom the account has not been properly conducted.

The London Gazette. This imposing publication gives details of county court judgements, bankruptcies, petitions for winding up and so on. The commercial reporting agencies normally extract this information and will supply it on a subscription basis.

Representatives' field reports frequently contain very useful current information because the compiler is one's own man who has certainly visited the premises and has come to know some if not all of the management. By careful internal liaison the credit manager can encourage and teach his field force to include in the reports useful details about the size and condition of the premises, the age and condition of the plant and machinery, a useful check against the valuation shown in the balance sheet. The quality of the stocks and the volume of the work-in-progress, an estimate of the number of employees and whether the place has an air of business-like efficiency about it.

The personal interview affords perhaps the best evaluation tool of all because the managing or financial director of the credit seeking company is met face-to-face.

Sales ledger control

Sales or debtors' ledger is the legal record of a company's trading transactions with its customers. Since it is these transactions which in the main generate the profits and the bad debts, it is essential that this ledger is regularly and accurately updated. Delay in writing up sales ledgers is the main cause of weakness in credit control. Unless the customer's account is up to date it is impossible to see the amount already at risk, or whether he has recently made a payment. Credit limits cannot be imposed effectively under these conditions.

The ledger should comprise a series of individual accounts, one for each customer. The practice of opening a "sundry sales account" should be avoided because such an account rapidly becomes a "dust-bin" and a means of by-passing the normal credit sanction procedures.

Legally, it is the duty of a debtor to seek out his creditor and pay the sum due on the due date. In practice, the creditor will be wise to send at the end of each month to every customer, a statement of account reflecting the unpaid balance, and the amount of that balance due and overdue.

The sales ledger should be updated daily by posting to the respective customer accounts every item of cash received, and every invoice raised. There will be occasions too when for one reason or another a customer will be given a credit note for perhaps faulty goods, a turn-over rebate, a pricing error, a contribution to advertising costs, etc. Such credit notes represent a reduction of the amount due from the customer and hence must be posted to the credit side of his account in the same way as cash received. It may also be the policy of the company to grant a "settlement discount"—perhaps "$2\frac{1}{2}\%$ monthly or $3\frac{3}{4}\%$ seven days." In such a case the net cash received will be for a lower value than that of the invoices paid to the extent of the discount taken. A journal entry is therefore necessary to debit this amount to cash discount and to credit the same amount to the customer's account in the sales ledger.

Frequently unscrupulous customers deduct the settlement discount even though the item or items being paid are overdue, ie have not been paid in accordance with the agreed credit terms. In such cases, the taken discount should be "disallowed" and the matter must be referred back to the customer by letter or telephone for settlement. Sometimes such a letter or telephone call will have the desired effect, more often the unscrupulous client will ignore the matter and in fact continue his practice of deducting a discount outside the settlement terms. A sub-stantial and virtually uncollectable balance accrues and the only remedy is to refer the matter to sales management as to whether or not they wish to continue trading with such a client or whether they are pre-pared to condone the practice and to take the "disallowed" discount as a sales expense.

The satisfactory operation of any credit control system relies upon a realistic credit limit being set for each customer and a comparison of this limit against the outstanding balance on the account at the time each order is processed for invoicing and dispatch. Unless each indi-vidual customer account is updated every day there would be no accur-ate balance available for this purpose. If the customer's balance at the time of order credit sanction does not reflect the latest cash received, it will be higher than it should be and could result in the order being rejected for credit limit reasons. Equally if all invoices are not posted to date the balance will show as less than it is in reality giving a margin against the credit limit that is apparently sufficient to allow the order to be passed by credit control. It will be seen therefore that unless there is available on the sales ledger an accurate up-to-the-minute picture of the client's account, credit sanction and credit limits cannot be satisfactorily operated. This would apply particularly in a busy integrated order-processing system as in a mail-order house or large retail store.

The sales ledger itself can, in its most simple form consist of a bound volume, one page per customer account, whereon are "hand-posted" the transactions. More usually it consists of trays of ledger cards, the entries on which are posted mechanically from a bookkeeping machine and its operator. The advantage of this system is that with each posting the outstanding balance is updated and the ledger-card constitutes a visual record of account experience. It is, however, a growing practice for the sales ledger to be maintained on a computer and for a daily, or twice daily run to record the transactions on disc or tape. At the end of each month the customer statements are printed out from the information stored daily and a copy of each of these statements becomes the working document for the sales ledger department.

The serious disadvantage of a computerised sales ledger is the fact that without filing a whole series of monthly statements there is not immediately available a visual record of a customer's account and one's experience thereon. The receivables program in the computer will normally provide for an interrogation facility to supply this information reasonably quickly. There is, however, inevitably some delay factor which can be of some embarrassment when one has a client on the end of a telephone awaiting a credit decision regarding a new order.

The traditional customer statement shows the outstanding balance brought forward from the previous month's transactions and the closing balance for the current month. It therefore reflects no history of the account and gives no analysis of the outstanding or unpaid items which comprise the opening balance. It is popular because it is easily and automatically produced by the bookkeeping machine as each entry is posted to the ledger card. If the sales ledger is hand-posted, then the monthly statements must be separately and individually produced each month. A statement of this type has too the disadvantage that "arithmetic" is necessary before any further information is available from it.

SALES LEDGER WORK SLIP								

The Client Limited
220 High Street
Anytown

Month ending				
Payment terms		Discount		
Credit limit				
Experience				

AGED ANALYSIS OF BALANCE			REMITTANCE ALLOCATION ON MONTHLY O/S BALANCES			CASH RECEIVED DURING CURRENT MONTH		
Month	Amount		Reference	Cash	Updated balance	Reference	Date	Balance

DIARY NOTES ON COLLECTION/CLEARING ACTION				
Date	Contact	Object of inquiry		Result of inquiry

FIGURE 7:3   SALES LEDGER WORK-SLIP

This particular form of monthly advice to a customer of the amount due, is perfectly adequate where the custom of the trade is to "pay to statement," that is to pay each month the amount shown on the statement as the closing balance and to negotiate and adjust any differences subsequently.

This practice is, however, becoming less and less practical as purchase ledger systems and controls become more sophisticated. Debtors more usually pay only after invoices have been cleared by a thorough check on price, quality, delivery, rebate, technical specification etc, a process which can and often does, in some trades, take some weeks and often months.

It is essential that, at all times, there is available an analysis of the individual items which make up the outstanding balance, "aged" into their respective months of original posting. With the type of statement now under discussion, the information regarding unpaid or uncleared items can be obtained only by referring back to the filed statements—a time-consuming procedure which does not produce a quick reference for dealing with telephoned enquiries. It is therefore advisable to attach to each current month's statement, a "work-slip" of some sort. This work-slip will be up-dated as each payment is received or as any item is cleared so that at all times there is available an "ageing" of the account. A specimen of such a work-slip is shown in Figure 7:3. It is vital however that each account balance is readily identifiable in its component parts and into the months each part has been outstanding. Wherever this routine is neglected, the customer is given the advantage that it is "his balance" which must be taken as the correct one for the simple reason that you, the creditor, cannot prove otherwise. The creditor, would be "on the wrong foot" and it could cost money.

The end product of all the computerised sales ledger operations is a record on the computer file of every new invoice produced and of every invoice paid plus sundry other information. Because each invoice paid is deleted from the record, those that remain on file represent at all times those still outstanding and it is this record which when printed out gives what is known as the open item statement.

The open item statement obviates the need for reconciliation, for retention of previous statements, for work-slips and so on. It gives a clear accurate picture of the outstanding situation on any customer's account and because of the ageing shown at the foot of the statement and the other transaction codes quoted on it, further control statistics become readily available. The "open item statement" is by far the most efficient method of maintaining a sales ledger.

At the close of each month there is a simple control mechanism which must be checked to prove the accuracy of the sales ledger operations for the month.

The accounts department will have produced a control calculation on the following lines:

Trade debtors at 30 June	120 000
Add sales for July per sales day book	200 000
	320 000
Deduct sales cash received per day book	230 000
Trade debtors at 31 July	90 000

Thus the total of the individual customer balances on the sales ledger should also be £90 000. If they do not come to this figure something has gone wrong and the error *must* be found before proceeding with posting the next month's transactions. To leave over agreement with the control figure is to invite even greater subsequent trouble.

Marginal costing in credit control

The credit controller should examine his company's marginal costing as a guide to deciding on safety standards. A bad debt, if it happens, is a straight loss equal to the difference between the amount of the debt and the margin of contribution included in the sale which created that debt.

The larger the ratio of contribution to sales, the bigger the risk the company is justified in taking.

To follow this argument and put it to practical use, it is first necessary to look at the theory of marginal costing which uses the formula $U(S-V) = F + P$.

U = number of units sold
S = sales price per unit
V = variable expenses directly related to each one unit
Contribution = $S - V$
F = fixed costs in total
P = profit

C.W.C.—F

	A	B
	£	£
Selling price per unit (S)	100	100
Variable costs per unit (V)	70	20
Contribution to fixed costs & profit (C)	30	80

$U = 1\ 000$ units sold during the period

	A	B
$U(S–V) =$	30 000	80 000
Fixed costs (F)	25 000	75 000
Net profit 5% of turnover (P)	£5 000	£5 000

FIGURE 7:4   CONTRASTING PROPORTIONS OF FIXED AND
VARIABLE COSTS

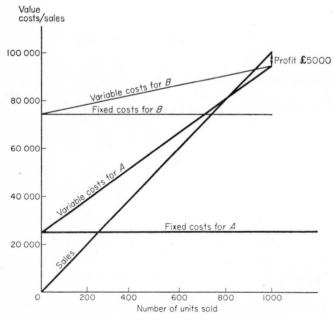

FIGURE 7:5   BREAK-EVEN CHART

Figure 7:4 shows two companies which have identical selling price and net profit when production and sales are at normal levels, but whose expenses show a totally different pattern. Company *A* relies heavily on variable costs and has few fixed costs, whilst company *B* has a solid block of fixed costs but its variable costs per unit are extremely small.

They have identical results with a fixed amount of sales, but a considerable difference when the volume of sales changes.

Figure 7:5 shows the effect of a marginal rise or fall of 5% in the number of units sold. A variation in level of sales greater than 5% could render a break-even chart of this type unreliable, because neither the fixed nor variable costs are perfectly true to their definition. However, within this limit of plus or minus 5%, the principle is sound. Each company would have to decide on the extent to which a change in the volume of sales could be made without seriously distorting the nature of fixed and variable costs.

	A	B
Selling price per unit (*S*)	100	100
Variable costs per unit (*V*)	70	20
	£	£
Contribution per unit (*S–V*)	30	80
Contribution from 10 units	300	800
Deduct the fixed overheads (*F*)	Nil	Nil
Balance adding to profit, before allowing for bad debts (*P*)	300	800
Failure rate—3 customers in 10 become total bad debts	*A*	*B*
Proceeds of sales should be	1000	1000
Proceeds are in fact	700	700
Variable costs created in making those sales	(10 × £70) 700	(10 × £20) 200
Total addition to net profit	0	500

FIGURE 7:6   ADDING 10 NEW CUSTOMERS WHO ARE POOR RISKS

Figure 7:6 shows the effect of adding ten units (10%) to the sales by agreeing to sell to customers who are classified by the credit controller as a poor risk. He would not accept them at all if they were a bad risk and his own judgement must help him distinguish between poor and bad.

In this example bad debts have completely cancelled the extra profit which would have been made by company *A* from the extra sales. This is the company whose variable costs are very high in proportion to its selling prices.

In company *B* the same failure rate amongst customers has still left an addition of £500 to the profit. So the risk-taking has been a very lucrative venture for *B*, whilst it was a complete waste of effort for *A*.

If the bad debts had proved even heavier, with four customers failing, company *A* would have been out of pocket, and made a loss on the deal, whilst *B* would still have been making £400 profit.

Before deciding on the risk-taking policy, the management should consider whether the extra sales are required in the light of availability of goods, staff and processing/handling facilities. To accept risky orders when the factory is already at the peak of its capacity is a pointless exercise because it means that if these orders are fulfilled, the established safe customer must be kept waiting. This throws the whole marginal concept adrift, because the extra orders are not turned into extra turnover so the units delivered to the doubtful customers would have been required to contribute towards fixed overheads and, so far as the bad debts are concerned, they have failed to do so.

When sales are below factory capacity

In times of tough competition, the failure to sell to normal customers leads to the idea of approaching potential new customers, whose willingness to buy is likely to be inversely proportional to their ability to pay.

To keep the factory going and cover overhead expenses, even if not making a profit, is a fair ambition if there is hope of better times ahead. Meanwhile, how can the credit controller contribute by his willingness to accept orders from shaky customers? The same theory of marginal costing will apply to this situation.

The smaller the proportion of variable costs per unit to sales price per unit the bigger the risk that will be justified.

In Figure 7:7 it has proved impossible to sell more than 800 units to established sound customers, compared to a normal level of 1000 units.

Actual sales to established sound
  customers   800 units
Sales to high-risk customers 200 units

Normal output   1000

	A	B
Failure—customers for 50 units fail to pay		
Fixed costs as in Figure 7:4	25 000	75 000
Variable costs, 1000 units produced @ £70	70 000 @ £20	20 000
	95 000	95 000
Actual sales income—950 units @ £100	95 000	95 000
Profit	0	0
OR		
Fixed costs	25 000	75 000
Variable costs, 800 units produced @ £70	56 000 @ £20	16 000
	81 000	91 000
Actual sales income, no bad debts 800 @ £100	80 000	80 000
Loss	1 000	11 000

FIGURE 7:7   CHOICE BETWEEN NORMAL AND REDUCED
SALES

The choice has been to stick to 800 units or to sell the other 200 units to high-risk customers.

It has made very little difference to company *A* with its high variable and low fixed costs that output has dropped by 20 per cent. Meanwhile *B* has seen a serious loss and would have done much better to sell to the high-risk customers.

Part Four
Management of Stocks

8

Establishing a Policy for Stock Control

Stocks are a necessary evil of the industrial and commercial world, and few companies would carry them if they were not absolutely essential to their survival.

Cost and classes of stocks

As a component part of working capital, stocks are probably one of the most difficult assets to control. They are costly at any level and their main effects can be seen in three different areas of costs:

1 The cost of finance equal to interest charges on funds borrowed to pay for the stock.
2 The cost of physically taking care of the stock, including storage space, security measures, handling equipment and the wages of warehouse staff.
3 The cost of writing down the value of stock. This may be due to deterioration, change of fashion, obsolescence or reduction in market value.

With many alternative uses to which funds must be allocated, the cost of stocks is a sensitive area in the management of working capital. When the company is short of funds in meeting all its needs, each additional £100 absorbed on the purchase of stocks may reduce the amount available for other uses. Such a situation is illustrated in Figure 8:1.

The present position of the business is shown in the first column of Figure 8:1. Business is brisk and the opportunity to raise £800 000 of

PRESENT POSITION		FORECAST	ACTUAL
£'000		£'000	£'000
400	Fixed assets	1 000	600
600	Stocks	800	1 200
500	Debtors	500	500
1 500	Total assets = total	2 300	2 300
	available funds		

FIGURE 8:1   CONTRAST BETWEEN FORECAST AND ACTUAL
USE OF INCREASED FUNDS

additional funds is seen as a good chance to expand profitable business
by installing extra plant at a cost of £600 000 and carrying £200 000 of
extra stocks.

The funds have been duly raised but instead of the full amount of
plant being acquired, much of the new funds have been diverted to pay
for a large unplanned rise in the stocks. Poor stock control has led to
funds earmarked for expansion of production facilities being used to
pay for stocks and the chance of increasing output has been restricted.

If the whole extra plant had already been ordered the position would
become dangerous with the sudden growth of £400 000 in unwilling
trade creditors, or non-agreed extension of the overdraft.

It might be argued that the extra machinery could be taken on lease
but this course of action is not always feasible. For example, this is not
possible if machines have been bought and paid for before the desperate
financial position has been understood. It is difficult (though perhaps
not quite impossible) to reverse a completed purchase transaction and
turn it into a lease agreement.

The function of the company's management is to estimate the optimum level of stocks to be held, taking into account all the circumstances.
To do this, in a manufacturing company, the stock should be evaluated
under three main headings: raw materials, work-in-progress and finished
goods. A wholesale or retail organisation holds only the third class.

1 *Raw materials.* This stock is held solely for the purpose of supplying
the factory with an uninterrupted flow of material at all times. A delay
of one day keeping the factory standing idle could mean a loss of
income far more serious than the cost of holding stocks equal to several
weeks' demand. It is the task of the purchasing officer to judge the

reliability of suppliers' delivery promises and to calculate the lead times so that stock may be cut fine without danger of running out.

Where the raw materials arise seasonally as, for example, foodstuffs at harvest time, the planning of stocks needs to take into account that the season's purchases must keep the factory supplied right through the next year. Close cooperation is needed between those responsible for buying the stocks and those who must arrange to find the funds to match the sudden rise in current assets. This will be a problem familiar to the executives working in this kind of business but they may not be so well aware of the need for planning their funds.

There may also be opportunities for buying extra stocks whilst prices are unusually low or to take advantage of seasonal fluctuations. Whether the company can afford to buy ten months' supply of raw material just because a seasonal glut has brought prices to a low level must depend upon the combined effect of borrowing costs and availability of funds apart from the physical problems of storage.

Here is a point in which the purchasing officer and raw materials stock controller may cooperate with the financial director in the management of the company's working capital by knowing when these exceptional chances of buying goods cheaply have arisen. The finance director in his turn will be ready to discover ways of raising the temporary funds equal to the increased stock.

2 *Work-in-progress.* It is a fair general proposition that work in progress is a nuisance best kept to the lowest possible level and that production executives make a fair contribution to the management of working capital simply by keeping it down. Incidentally, and perhaps more importantly, they generally find that management control of the production departments is strengthened by keeping control of this form of stock.

Exceptions to the general rule are:

(*a*) If work follows through several successive departments, it may be useful to hold a buffer stock of work in progress at each stage. For example, if departments *A*, *B* and *C* are all concerned with making product *Z*, stocks of partly processed material held at the entrance to *B* would help to mitigate the effect of a breakdown happening in *A*. A further stock at the entrance to *C* would help reduce the effect of a breakdown in *B*.

Experience is usually the best guide in assessing the risk of such breakdowns taking place.

Where production is for stock as distinct from meeting orders already in hand, the benefit of these departmental buffer stocks may be cancelled by the risk that the final product will fail to sell and yet there is little choice but to continue making it after this discovery until the buffer stocks have been cleared.

(b) Some partly made goods may be set aside to permit work to go ahead on orders more urgently required. This usually brings production problems although it may be highly attractive to salesmen seeking to please important customers.

3 *Stock of finished goods.* The nature of the business determines the need for holding this type of stock. The attractions of holding substantial stocks are:

(a) This may enable the factory to manufacture its products in long runs which is a very economical method of production.

(b) The sales staff have a wide range available to offer customers for prompt delivery.

The dangers are:

(a) A faulty decision in the type of stocks to be held may lead to absorbing funds and storage space for unsaleable or slow-moving lines.

(b) The company's funds may be strained beyond their limit.

On balance the dangers are likely to be far more serious than the advantages of holding stocks. The sales staff will generally make their best contribution towards management of working capital by learning to maintain good sales from minimum stocks.

The distribution executive also makes a valuable contribution to this effort by being unusually efficient in the movement of goods from the point of completion of their manufacture to their arrival at the customer's premises. If the average delay between these two points can be cut down from eight days to two days there will be an enormous saving in the amount of working capital tied up in the form of stocks. This executive has ensured that the goods cease to be stock and are translated into the form of trade debtors and the sooner they reach this point the sooner they are going to be translated again into the form of cash received from the customers.

Stock control objectives: a summary

1 *Raw material*
(a) Keeping stocks to a minimum compatible with never leaving the factory without supplies.
(b) Finding opportunities for buying extra supplies at favourable prices; the temporary rise in working capital being justified by the low costs.

2 *Work-in-progress*
(a) Keeping the stock in each department to the lowest possible level.
(b) Knowing when it is justifiable to hold buffer stocks between successive departments.

3 *Finished goods*
(a) The real skill is in keeping customers satisfied without actually having any goods in stock whatsoever.

	A	B
Production time	15 days	3 days
Stock of finished goods	£12 000	£2 000
Turnover	£72 000	£60 000*
Rate of stock turnover	6 times a year	30 times a year
Loss on finished goods which prove to be unsaleable	£2 000	£300
Net profit before stock losses and before charging interest on loans needed to pay for stock 10% of turnover	7 200	6 000
Interest on stock @ 10%	1 200	200
	6 000	5 800
Stock losses	2 000	300
Net profit	4 000	5 500

* Sales smaller because one-sixth of orders were missed through customers being unwilling to wait three days for delivery.

FIGURE 8:2 COMPARISON OF LARGE AND SMALL STOCKS OF FINISHED GOODS

Note: Company *B* with its close control on production and small stock of finished goods has accepted most orders for delivery and has finished with a 37% higher net profit

(b) Short of that almost impossible ideal (and depending on nature of the trade) the benefits of keeping the stocks to the lowest level reasonably possible will usually outweigh the possible benefits of holding larger stocks.

(c) Production managers will contribute towards success by maintaining a rapid flow through of goods to meet customers' specific orders. To offer a promise of delivery in three days, knowing the goods can be manufactured in that time, may satisfy customers who would not be willing to wait a fortnight. This point is brought out in Figure 8:2.

Holding no stocks of finished goods cuts out many risks.

Valuation of stocks

The value of stock is a matter of opinion, which preferaby should be based on experience and full knowledge of market conditions.

	A	B	C	
	NORMAL	HIGH	LOW	
Share capital	1000	1000	1000	The reserves form the cross entry, being directly
Reserves (including retained profit)	600	900	300	affected by the change in the
	1600	1900	1300	declared value of the stock
Long-term loans ⎫ Short-term loans ⎬	400	400	400	
	2000	2300	1700	
Stock	800	1100	500	
Debtors	500	500	500	
	1300	1600	1000	
less trade creditors	200	200	200	
Working capital	1100	1400	800	
Other assets	900	900	900	
	2000	2300	1700	

FIGURE 8:3   BALANCE SHEET WITH THREE VIEWS OF THE VALUE OF STOCK

A change in the valuation placed on stock makes an apparent difference to the funds employed in the company. This may mislead everyone cencerned with reading the company's balance sheet, and profit and loss account, including the directors, the accountants, the bank manager and the shareholders.

In Figure 8:3, column *A* shows the stock with its customary level of valuation and the reserves are £600. Column *B* shows an optimistic revaluation of the stock by £300 and in consequence the working capital appears to have increased by £300 and so have the reserves. Column *C* shows the opposite effect of a pessimistic cut of £300 in the stock valuation.

The amount which will actually be received from selling this stock may be:

1 Unchanged by the distorted valuation in either *B* or *C*, because price fixing for sales does not depend on the valuation. Therefore the true value of the working capital has not been altered from column *A* and the accounts presented by showing either column *B* or column *C* have simply given a wrong picture of the working capital and the reserves.

2 Increased as in column *B* because the selling prices are made to reflect the higher stocks and the customers are persuaded to pay the extra amounts. Therefore the revision of stock values and so of working capital has been genuine and has been to the company's benefit. Incidentally, the upwards revaluation of stock above its cost price would never be adopted in published accounts although it might well be used in internal management accounts.

3 Reduced as shown in column *C* because sales are achieved at these new lower levels whereas customers were reluctant to pay the prices demanded according to the normal level in column *A*. Again the revision of stock values and of working capital has been genuine and has been to the company's benefit because they have found price levels which have enabled them to clear these otherwise unwanted stocks.

The value placed on stock for preparation of the balance sheet, which sets the level at which it forms a part of the working capital, may be unsuitable for the other purposes, and several separate valuations of the stock will be needed. These include:

1 Insurance against fire and theft. Whereas the balance sheet uses "cost or market value, whichever is the lower" the insurance cover should always be at the higher of these two alternatives. The actual method of valuation must depend to some extent on the terms of the policy but generally it would be substantially above a balance sheet valuation at the same date. It would be further complicated by having to cover for the peak level which might not coincide with any balance sheet date.

TRADING ACCOUNT

Opening stock	10 units @ £40	400
Purchases	40 units @ £50	200
		2 400
Closing stock	10 units @ £50	500
		1 900
Sales	40 units @ £100	4 000
Gross profit		2 100
Other costs	40 units @ £40	1 600
Net profit		500

		Per unit
Sales	material	50
	other costs	40
		90
Profit		10
Selling price		100

40 units will show profit on this basis	= £400
Trading account shows profit as	500
"false" profit on disposal of opening stock	£100

FIGURE 8:4   FALSE PROFIT ON STOCK
DISPOSAL

Basic principle. Any increase in stock due to higher prices for similar goods reflects inflation and not a true growth in the asset in real terms. Comparisons of stocks from one year end to another are blurred by
this element

2 Costing for price fixing. In an economy where prices are rising constantly whether by regular steps or in erratic bursts, sound commercial practice is to arrange selling prices for the firm's products according to the projected cost price of materials during the period when the sales will be taking place.

Whilst both the trading account and the balance sheet will use a stock figure based on the lowest interpretation of its value, the costing system will ignore this and operate on the much higher level of replacement costs (see Figure 8:4).

The argument that the extra profit of £100 shown in Figure 8:4 came from selling the opening stock is founded on the inevitable way this £100 is tied up in a permanent addition to stock (and so to working capital). Without any more volume of stock being available for trading purposes this element of working capital has eaten up £100 which will never be released unless or until business is discontinued.

3 In the last resort it is a sound maxim of business that stock is worth what it will fetch. The company is always faced with the choice between selling at the best price obtainable or continuing to hold the stock until such time as trading conditions improve.

Funds tied up in stock which resolutely refuses to move are adding nothing to income but are continuing to incur further expense. Selling prices will be modified between the desirable levels in 2 above and the valuations used for balance sheet purposes—or even lower in drastic cases.

When stocks have been cleared at drastically reduced prices it must be recognised that the funds which have been tied up in them have been permanently lost to the extent of the difference between balance sheet valuation and disposal price. The problem of the management is to choose between early disposal at a loss and waiting in anticipation of improvements.

------------------ 9 ------------------

Principles of Stock Control

Stocks are a significant capital asset. Published accounts of large companies such as the General Electric Company Limited, for example, show stocks worth over one third of the total assets. For Turner and Newall Limited, stocks amount to just over one quarter of total assets.

These stocks consist essentially of stocks of materials and purchased parts, components or subassemblies of material and components in process in the factory, and of finished goods. In addition, stocks of subassemblies or partly finished products may be held in intermediate stores. In aggregate the value of all these stocks can be usefully described by the general term "inventory."

Inventory performance

In the final analysis, inventory performance is reflected in the overall profitability of the business. Not only does this item figure substantially in the denominator of the most widely accepted single yardstick by which any business is judged, namely the return on investment, but there are costs arising from the holding of stocks as such — storage, damage, loss, fire insurance, obsolescence and so on — apart from the cost represented by the capital tied up.

The most common measure of inventory performance is the ratio of the value of the inventory to annual sales as a percentage (or its inverse, the inventory turnover per year). For both companies referred to earlier, this ratio comes to approximately 30% and its inverse to 3.3 times per year. This cannot be said to be good or bad without some knowledge of the industry concerned; for a daily newspaper it would be appallingly poor, but for the forestry industry it might appear miraculously good.

Another useful measure of performance is the service level, closely related to stockout frequency. While these are more often applied to stocks of finished goods, they can be applied to stocks of materials, and with more difficulty to work-in-progress. It is possible to have too low a level of work-in-progress, leading to intermittent stoppages in different parts of the factory, with bad effects on overall efficiency.

Any such measures need precise definition, and considerable time can be spent in discussion of whether one definition is better than another.

A change of definition is the easiest way to achieve a substantial improvement in any measure, but it does not in general alter the underlying reality. If the inventory performance is poor, by any reasonable standard, this must indicate lack of control somewhere. Lack of inventory control indicates lack of production control.

Control of stocks

In most companies, any increase in the value of the fixed assets or plant, as for example by the purchase of a new lathe, has to be justified by a full exposition of the advantages to be gained from such an acquisition, the total costs involved, other possible alternative means of achieving the same results and so on. Yet the expenditure of a similar sum of money on an increase in stocks often requires no such formal justification; the signature of a stock control clerk, in many cases, is all that is required. For effective use of working capital this is clearly not good enough, and it is necessary to explore, in just as much detail, the means whereby the levels of stocks are kept under control. Deliberate control is essential, in place of the frequently occurring situation where the stock levels seem to arise more or less as an inevitable consequence of the day-to-day decisions taken with very little policy guidance from the higher levels of management.

For this to be done intelligently, and for clear directives to be issued, a definition of the purposes for which stocks are being held, the ways in which these can save the company money, the costs of having these stocks and of looking after them, must all be explicitly examined in considerable detail. The outcome should be used to formulate simple unambiguous directives as the basis of stock control policy.

Suitable stock control systems can then be built up embodying these principles, allowing sufficient scope for the stock control staff to exercise their own particular skills, knowledge and experience to get good results, but still within the framework of the management policy.

Reasons for holding stocks

A retail business, a wholesale business, a supply undertaking (except for electricity, perhaps) must all have stocks of the goods they sell or supply. Hotels must have stocks of food, service organisations stocks of replacement parts, and manufacturing industries need stocks of:

1 Raw materials and purchased parts
2 Intermediate parts, subassemblies, or assemblies
3 Finished goods ready for shipment and sale

If there is no definite plan to provide these and control them, stocks will arise through the normal operations of the business; moreover, the forces tending to increase the stock holding are usually more direct in operation, and hence more effective, than those tending to limit the stocks. A satisfactory plan calls for a thorough understanding of the processes involved, the various pressures concerned, and the responsibilities of each part of management in relation to stocks, together with a set of firm policies, clearly defined and delineated, and the appropriate controls and reporting mechanisms.

Information flow

Figures 9:1, 9:2, 9:3 and 9:4 show the flow of information, orders, designs and instructions as well as material at all stages of manufacture, in a typical manufacturing business. The details will differ from business to business, but the general pattern remains the same.

Customer's order. The complex flow-pattern is most easily followed stage by stage from the receipt of a customer's order.

If the order is for a product whose design is known, and if there are adequate stocks, the order can be supplied ex-stock.

If the product is known, but cannot be supplied from stock, the requirement is passed to production control to be scheduled.

An order for a new product, if accepted, leads to a new design, and then to a requirement for manufacture. The new design must be examined for:

1   How to make the product (manufacturing layouts)
2   What to make it from (parts lists)
3   How much of each resource (man-hours, machine-hours), is needed per unit of finished goods

If any stocks of finished goods are held these will need to be replenished from time to time, with due regard for future forecast requirements. There are thus three possible sources of requirements for manufacture:

1   A repeat order that cannot be met from stock
2   An order for a new product
3   Replenishments for finished goods stock

These requirements must be combined and presented to the scheduling section of production control, as shown in Figure 9:1.

Master schedule. The scheduling section (see Figure 9:2) prepares a master schedule on the basis of:

1   The requirements for finished goods
2   The available plant capacity
3   The resources needed to make each product
4   The availability of the required materials

The master schedule lists each product, with the quantities of each product to be made in each of a series of successive periods.

Gross explosion

For fairly simple products, it is then straightforward to determine the materials and parts needed to enable this schedule to be met, using the parts list for each product, by the process known as gross explosion. The quantity of each material or component part per product is multiplied by the number of that product required, with due allowance for the process time involved.

Allowance for any existing stocks of parts or material is made in a gross to net calculation, and any necessary orders can be placed for purchase or manufacture.

Net explosion, level by level

For complex products, there are often stocks of intermediate assemblies

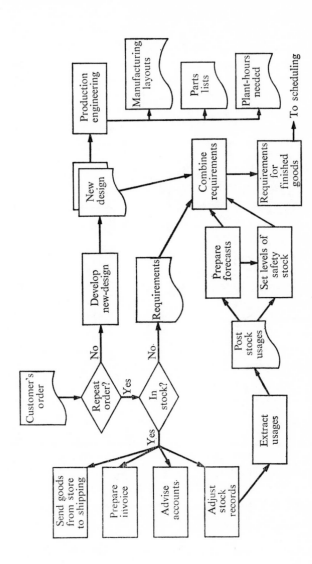

FIGURE 9:1 FLOW OF INFORMATION FROM CUSTOMER'S ORDER TO REQUIREMENTS FOR FINISHED GOODS

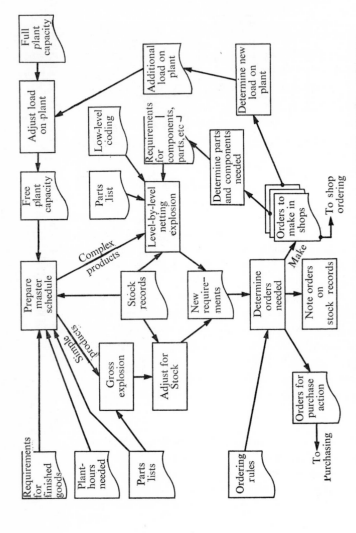

FIGURE 9:2   FROM FINISHED GOODS TO ORDERS TO MAKE OR BUY

and subassemblies, and gross explosion followed by netting becomes clumsy. The modern motor car provides a ready example. It is assembled from:

1 A body
2 A set of wheels
3 An engine
4 A transmission system

Each of these is itself an assembly of component parts. For example, the engine has already been built up from the basic engine block, its head, pistons and valves, a starter motor, a generator, a distributor and so on. Dissection need not stop here; for the distributor is itself a complex product.

Level-by-level explosion is an iterative process. All finished products are referred to as belonging to level 0. They are assembled from sub-assemblies which belong to level 1; these subassemblies themselves may be put together from sub-subassemblies (level 2), some of which are made from other parts (level 3), and so on. Products which can be exploded through twenty levels are not at all rare in engineering.

The determination of requirements for parts by level explosion consists of taking the requirements for a finished product (level 0), producing from it the requirements for its component parts at level 1, subtracting from these the known or planned stocks to get the net requirements at level 1, and then proceeding to level 2 and lower levels stage by stage.

Orders for purchase or manufacture are initiated based on these requirements following the prescribed ordering rules.

Orders for purchased items

Any orders for purchase are sent to the purchasing department for action as in Figure 9:3.

The purchasing department acts on these orders by selecting a supplier, negotiating price, delivery and perhaps quality standards with him, and then issuing a purchase order. The supplier may offer more favourable terms for a bigger order; this should always be referred to the stock controller. 1000 parts at 2p each are not a bargain, compared with 600 parts at 3p each, if there is no reasonable prospect of using or selling the other 400 when only 600 are needed.

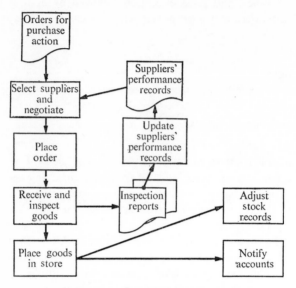

FIGURE 9:3   PURCHASING CYCLE

Orders for parts to be made

The manufacturing requirements are examined for the component parts needed (which may call for a further level of explosion), and for the work load on the factory plant; the relevant shop documents are then prepared (Figure 9:4).

Shop documents include instructions to the stores to issue materials, as well as detailed instructions about the operations to be carried out on these materials. After each operation, job tickets may report the work done, the time taken, the operator's name, and other details.

Rejects may arise at any inspection stage; some of these may be re-worked, some may be worth taking apart to recover component parts, while the remainder will have to be scrapped. All this will affect the final quantity delivered to store, and in any business where the pro-portion of rejects is normally appreciable (and there are some flourish-ing businesses where the ultimate yield is low but acceptable), the fluctuations of reject percentage from batch to batch can itself lead to more finished products being made than are needed. This is another potential source of stocks, overmakes, even where the policy is normally against holding stocks.

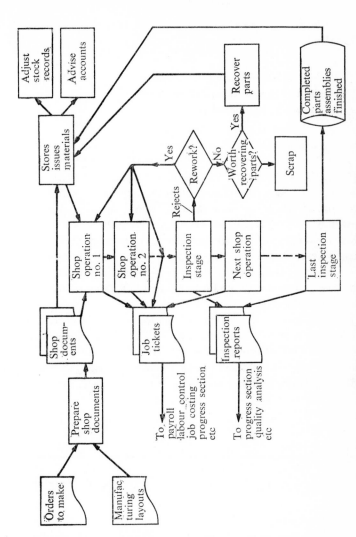

FIGURE 9:4 FROM SHOP ORDERING TO COMPLETION OF WORK

How stocks arise

From the flow charts in Figures 9:1 to 9:4, it is possible to see how stocks arise in three areas:

1   Finished goods including overmakes
2   Subassemblies and manufactured parts
3   Materials and purchased parts

Finished goods. Stocks of finished goods can be held as a deliberate policy, or they can arise as part of the normal running of the business.

Salesmen find that early delivery is a powerful factor in obtaining an order in the face of competition. Price, performance, and quality being more or less equal, or at least balanced, the order will go to the man who can offer the quicker delivery, preferably ex-stock.

Most production units bemoan the prevalence of short runs. The efficiency never builds up; the tempo is never really established, and so on. There is, too, the inevitable loss of production capacity of a machine each time it is set up for a different job. Long runs can only be achieved by holding stocks.

Where the demand is seasonal (as in the cases of swimwear, diaries, and television sets, to name but a few) there can be a widely fluctuating demand for manufacturing capacity, with alternating problems of recruitment and redundancy, unless a deliberate policy is followed of steady production, building up stocks to meet the peak demand.

Overmakes. Surpluses of finished goods can arise from cancellation of an order, or from a higher yield than was expected from a particular manufactured batch. The surplus, overmakes, can be stocked in the hope of a future demand which it can meet, either directly or with some modification which would still be quicker or cheaper than making from the start.

Subassemblies and manufactured parts. It may be accepted practice in the industry to offer short delivery (perhaps one month) but not immediate delivery, and this can be achieved by holding stocks of parts and subassemblies prior to final assembly. Such stocks provide extra flexibility, as many varieties of each finished product can be offered based on the same subassembly or building blocks.

Materials and purchased parts. Of all the stocks these are the most easily comprehended. No manufacturing business can operate without stocks of the appropriate materials. Such stocks can:

1   Allow the day-to-day demands by the factory to be met independently of the frequency of delivery by the suppliers
2   To some extent, provide a cushion against interruptions in the supply for any reason
3   Reduce the ordering costs
4   Reduce the price paid, as suppliers will often give a discount on larger quantities purchased
5   Even help to meet delivery dates, if the materials themselves are long-delivery items

10

Stock Control in Action

Elements of control

In the last thirty years there have been great developments in the field
of control engineering. The underlying principles are simple. To control
anything it is necessary to follow the essential steps shown in Figure 10:1.

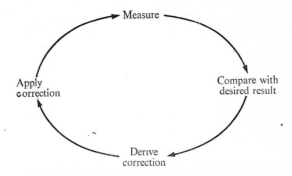

FIGURE 10:1   BASIC CONTROL CYCLE

1   The thing to be controlled must be measurable, and it must
    be measured
2   The measured value must be compared with a desired (or
    standard) result, which may be fixed or may change from
    time to time
3   The comparison yields a difference, usually referred to as the
    error, and from this a correction is derived
4   The correction is applied to the process
5   A new measurement is made, starting the process cycle again.

This all takes time, and in the meantime a number of things may have happened:

1   The outside environment may have changed, causing changes to the quantity itself
2   The standard may have changed
3   The system will have begun to respond to the correction applied to it

The cycle repeats itself, either until a specific end result has been achieved, or as a continuing process maintaining a desired condition.

Control applied to stocks

To control stocks, the same principles are applied (see Figure 10:2). Some preliminary steps are necessary:

1   The stocks and stock items must be identified
2   The units of stock, and how these are to be measured, must be decided
3   There must be rules about which items are to be stocked
4   The consequence of a stockout must be assessed for each item

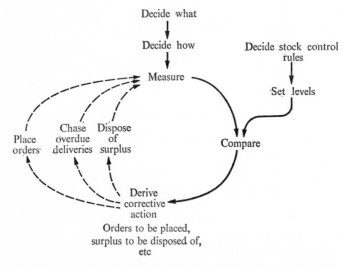

FIGURE 10:2   CONTROL CYCLE APPLIED TO STOCKS

5   Control levels can then be set, appropriate to whatever stock
     control system has been selected

With these preliminary steps accomplished, it is possible to:

1   Measure the actual stock level of each item
2   Compare this level with the control levels
3   Decide what should be done
4   Initiate this action (and follow up as necessary)

Control applied to inventory

While the control cycle for individual items is at the heart of stock
control, it is also necessary to look at the overall position of all the
stocks, and the money they represent. This is, in a sense, a summarising
of the position for all the items. There may be some thousands of items
to consider, so that some form of aggregate view is essential.

As mentioned in Chapter 9, the term "inventory" is conveniently
used to describe the aggregate value of all items and classes of physical
stocks.

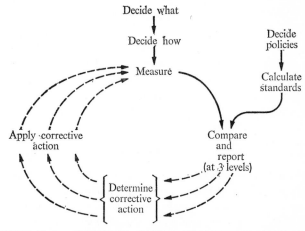

FIGURE 10:3   CONTROL CYCLE APPLIED TO INVENTORY

Figure 10:3 shows the control cycle applied to overall inventory
control. The same four preliminary steps must be taken, but the
corrective action now takes a different form. It is based largely on
reports, and these stimulate action in appropriate areas. Though not

shown on the Figure, the reports may themselves prompt alterations in the policies and rules set for individual stock items, and hence the standards set.

What to measure

In the case of inventory control, the decision about what to measure reflects the need to classify stock items so that a meaningful summary, in money terms, can be produced. Each class must have its own account ledger, so that the more classes there are, the higher the accounting costs, but the better the degree of control.

Inventory reports and corrective action

The error or differences between the actual and the standard levels can usefully be reported at three levels of management:

1   Stock controller level
2   Middle management
3   Top management

—all on a selective basis, so that only the more significant differences are reported to the higher levels. The reports at each level should summarise the position for the classes of stock for which the manager or supervisor is responsible.

The recipient of the report will decide upon appropriate action. The first line of defence is the stock controller. If the deviations are beyond his control, the production controller may have to act; in extreme cases, the attention of the manager will be drawn to the cases which only he can cope with.

Cost of control

At all times it must be borne in mind that precision costs money. Expensive items are worth controlling tightly; the same degree of control on penny items is extravagant. The cost of control should be balanced against the costs arising from any lack of control. The loss of one or two cheap items is of very little consequence unless their absence causes a significant hold up in production. It is well to err on the side of having too many of such an item.

In many cases, high precision is not even worth aiming at. The study of order costs shows that the total costs associated with the optimal conditions are only slightly increased by fairly large departures from these conditions. This justifies, to a large extent, a number of approximations which make it impossible to describe stock control as a precise process, yet the advantages to be gained from such an imprecise process are very great indeed.

Basic steps towards good stock control

Good stock control depends upon the availability of good data and the choice of an appropriate system. Above all, though, there is a paramount need for people to know and understand the system and their own responsibilities and limits within that system.

The one-man business may have problems of stock control, but there is never any doubt about who must tackle these problems. On the other hand, reference to Figures 9:1 to 9:4 will quickly show that in a manufacturing business of any appreciable size there are a number of areas where different people have different interests, and where responsibilities must be allocated and defined if serious conflict is not to arise.

The three main areas of potential conflict, as far as stock control is concerned, are:

1   The ordering of materials or components from suppliers
2   The ordering of components or subassemblies from the factory
3   The stocking of finished goods or of intermediate assemblies

Figure 10:4 shows a simplified organisation structure which may be used to illustrate these points.

Purchased items

When the stock of a purchased item runs low, the stock controller will decide on a quantity to be ordered, using any rules that have been set down and his knowledge of future requirements and past usages, and with due regard for storage problems and the importance of minimising stock holding costs. He will specify a delivery date, and will request the purchasing department to make appropriate arrangements with a supplier.

The buyer in the purchasing department has a detailed knowledge of his suppliers and of the general state of the supply market. He may be able to predict a forthcoming shortage of some commodity, or a growing overload situation among suppliers of certain specialised components. A supplier may offer him a lower unit price for a larger

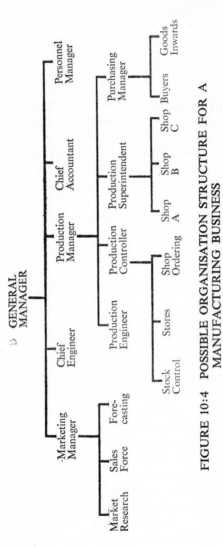

FIGURE 10:4 POSSIBLE ORGANISATION STRUCTURE FOR A
MANUFACTURING BUSINESS

order. He has thus many good reasons for ordering more than he has been asked to. Should he do so? Or is this outside his area of responsibility? If he increases the order, the stock of this material will rise, and the stock controller may be criticised for tying up too much capital. Clearly, a definition of responsibility is required.

In some cases, the organisation structure itself resolves the difficulty. If, for example, the stock control of purchased materials and components is carried out within the purchasing department, the purchasing manager obviously has the full responsibility. But this means at least two separate stock control centres, and introduces other problems. What, for example, is done when a component is sometimes bought, and sometimes made, depending on the load in the factory? Rules known to be acceptable and to work are:

1 The stock controller is responsible for the level of his stocks.
2 Therefore he must control the quantity ordered.
3 The buyer—or the purchasing manager—is free to negotiate with any supplier and should in any case keep in touch with the market. He may, indeed should, suggest to the stock controller a change of the ordered quantity wherever he sees a real advantage for the business.
4 The stock controller and the buyer should discuss the reasons, with due regard for the money value of the order and the time taken up by the discussions.
5 The stock controller must make the ultimate decisions, bearing in mind the factors involved.

Manufacturing costs
Similar considerations enter into the placing of an order on the factory. The factory prefers long runs; efficiency rises; the loss of productive capacity due to machine set-up is reduced; but stocks will increase. The responsibility should still rest with the stock controller, but he should take due note of the factory viewpoint.

Finished goods made for stock
The problem of responsibility for finished goods can be the thorniest of all, because of the different ways by which an item can find its way into finished stock:

1 Goods made ahead of a scheduled delivery date to fill a trough in the work load of a production shop.
2 A customer can request a deferment of an order, or even cancel it, too late for this to be reflected in the manufacturing schedule.

3 Goods can be in transit waiting for suitable packaging, documentation or transport.

4 As an overmake, arising from a batch with a higher than average yield.

5 An authorised stock to meet a forecast demand.

6 As part of an economic manufacturing batch, the remainder having been sold.

The following are good working rules for this situation:

1 Where the general policy is to make goods only against a specific order, finished goods should be the responsibility of the production department, except for any deliveries deferred at the customer's request.

2 Where the policy is to make goods for stock, they should be the responsibility of the marketing department, to whom a separate finished goods stock controller should report.

11

Stock Recording and Classification

The stock controller needs a clear, unambiguous set of records. Where a computer is in use, these records may be kept on a reel of magnetic tape or a magnetic disc, but they still exist as the authoritative source of information.

Subsidiary records should be discouraged. Some organisations have stock record cards, bin cards in the store, accounting records in the accounts department, and even records of stock in purchasing, and a great deal of time is wasted trying to reconcile the balances on the various records.

Identification of stock items

All materials, components, parts and subassemblies should be given a part number, identifying that part specifically, no matter which end product it goes into. Part numbers can be simply numerical or they can be made to convey a certain amount of information about the shape of a part, the material from which it is made, its end use or various other factors which may be required for grouping or analysis purposes.

Check digits. With simple numerical coding, errors in transcription can easily be made. This risk can be substantially reduced by the addition of one or more extra digits of the code number, in such a manner as to point out the more common transcription errors. A very simple example of a check digit calculation is to add the digits of the code number together, and to take the last digit of the sum as the check digit.

A great deal of work has been done on such coding, known generally as redundancy coding, in the fields of information transfer, data transmission, and computers, directed at getting the maximum insurance against errors for a given expenditure in extra digits to be transmitted.

Stock classification

Stocks must be classified, not only for better control, but also for other reasons. The first division is by manufacturing stages, into:

1   Pre-process stocks
2   Intermediate stocks
3   Finished goods

Pre-process stocks. These are the stocks which have not yet been worked in the factory under consideration. They may be further subdivided into:

1   Raw material from which parts are to be made
2   Purchased parts
3   Purchased assemblies
4   Consumable materials (solder, cleaning materials, etc)
5   Consignment stocks (these will be discussed below)
6   Reserved material (also to be discussed below)

Consignment stocks. In general, all stocks on a factory site are part of the inventory. The case of consignment stocks provides the only exception.

Many firms have a number of materials or components where the annual value is extremely high. Among these there may be a limited number where there are only two or three suppliers, with comparable prices, quality and delivery. One of these, possibly, would be willing, in return for a majority share of the business, to keep a stock inside his customer's store, still acknowledged as part of the supplier's inventory. Such a stock is said to be on consignment.

The supplier gains free storage space and an edge over his competitors; the customer avoids having money tied up yet has ready access to the stock.

Reserved material. This is a special category of pre-process stock, where the manufacturing programme and the necessary routines are available for the material to be set aside, or reserved, for a particular order or job.

Intermediate stocks. These consist of parts and subassemblies which have been made or processed in the shop, all destined to have further work done on them before they can be regarded as finished goods, ready for sale.

Finished goods. These are, as the term implies, stocks of goods ready for sale or for dispatch to a customer.

Slow-moving, obsolescent and dead stock

All sections of stock will contain, unfortunately, a proportion of slow-moving, obsolescent and dead stock. These are often regarded as almost synonymous terms, but they are better distinguished as, perhaps:

1   *Slow-moving*: existing stock would last for two years or more at the current rate of usage, but is still expected to be used up
2   *Obsolescent*: existing stock in danger of being rendered obsolete by an imminent design change or by market conditions
3   *Dead stock*: existing stock for which no further demand can be foreseen

If any slow-moving item comes up for a replenishment order to be placed by the normal operation of a stock control system, the reorder level clearly needs revision.

Obsolescent stock is, as its name implies, in danger of becoming dead stock. No further orders should be placed, and if current stocks have appreciable value it may be worth considering alternative uses or disposal of at least some of this stock at once.

Dead stock is dead. It figures in the inventory detail; it occupies space; it represents money spent that cannot now be realised. Once identified, it should be disposed of, preferably by conversion to other uses or by sale at bargain prices.

Classification by usage value and *ABC*

One of the most fruitful ways of classifying stocks is by usage value or *ABC*.

The nineteenth-century Italian philosopher, Pareto, pointed out that a very large part of all the wealth in Italy was owned by a small proportion of the people. He drew a curve, similar in shape to that in

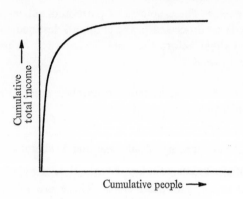

FIGURE 11:1   PARETO CURVE,
RELATING INCOME TO PEOPLE

Figure 11:1, by first ranking people in terms of their wealth, and then plotting the cumulative total wealth for the top person, then the top two, the top three, and so on.

It was Ford Dickie, in America, who adopted this approach to analysing stocks some twenty years ago, calling the technique *ABC*. The steps are simple:

1   For each item of any store, the average usage value in pounds per week, or other convenient units of money and time, is calculated
2   A list of these items is made, with the item having the highest usage value first, the next highest second, the next highest third, and so on
3   Opposite each item on the list is put its usage value
4   Cumulative totals of the numbers of items, and of the usage values, are made
5   These are turned into percentages of the total number of items and of the total usage value respectively
6   The percentages are plotted as shown in Figure 11:2. Three typical curves are illustrated

On this basis, it is possible to divide the stock items into three classes, *A*, *B* and *C*, such that:

A items are 10% of the items, and account for 60% of the total usage value.

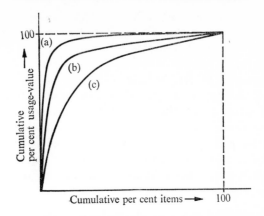

FIGURE 11:2   CUMULATIVE USAGE VALUE, PLOTTED AGAINST
THE CUMULATIVE NUMBER OF ITEMS
IN STOCK

B items are the next 30% of the items and account for 30% of the total
usage value.

C items are the remaining 60% of the items, and account for only
10% of the total usage value.

The exact percentages will vary from case to case, but the above are
typical. Clearly there are benefits to be obtained by treating *A* items,
B items and *C* items in different ways.

If the *A* items are controlled very closely (only 10% of all items), 60%
of the money is under strict control. At the other end of the scale,
controls on the *C* items can be much less stringent, except in one very
important respect—the danger of running out of stock. A stockout on
a *C* item can be as disastrous as on an *A* item, if it precludes the completion and shipment of an expensive finished product.

The important point is that different means of control can be used
to achieve similar degrees of protection from stockouts. For *A* items,
this can be obtained by careful attention to each individual item; for
C items, by having large amounts of safety stock.

Concentration on the *A* items can help in other ways. Two examples
come from the field of inventory reduction, a need for which can arise
in any company at some time or other:

1 *A* items are, more often than not, items with long lead times. This
means that *A* items are ordered well in advance, and in the interval

between the order and the arrival of the item, market conditions can change, reschedules can occur, and there may even be a change of design of the product to be made from this item. It may happen that an order placed in March, for a batch of material to be delivered in September, could be reviewed in August and shown to be not needed until November. If the supplier is agreeable, delivery can be deferred, saving inventory. A review of this kind could not be done economically for all items, but can pay handsomely if applied to A items alone.

2 At the other end of the factory, in the finished goods store, there are A, B and C items too. If a drive is to be made to sell off, or otherwise dispose of, slow moving stock, attention should once again be concentrated on the A items.

Costs of holding stock

Stock control involves the balance between economical production, quick delivery and low inventory value. If this is to be done constructively, as many as possible of the conflicting interests must be expressed in a common unit; the best available is money. Thus costs must be

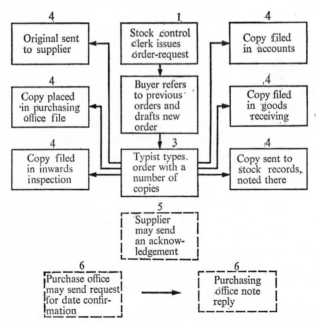

FIGURE 11:3   STEPS INVOLVED IN PLACING AN ORDER

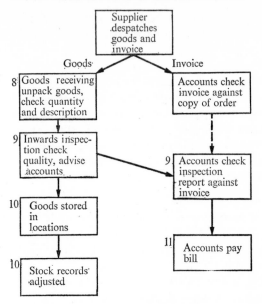

FIGURE 11:4   STEPS INVOLVED IN RECEIVING AND PAYING
FOR A DELIVERY

evaluated somehow; even if some of the values have to be subjective
and approximate.

Ordering and delivery costs. These are best taken together, as the delivery
costs are usually included in the order costs.

The steps involved in placing an order are shown in Figure 11:3 and
those for receiving a delivery in Figure 11:4.

The stock control clerk requests that an order should be placed.
He transmits this to the purchasing department by filling in a purchase
order request form. The appropriate buyer will select a supplier and
write out an order, which has then to be typed, probably as a set of
documents with copies for accounts, purchasing, goods receiving,
inwards inspection and stock control departments. If the supplier
sends an acknowledgement of the order this will be noted in the files.

All these steps cost money; some of them may be omitted in certain
cases, and they vary from one business to another.

Schedules and call-off deliveries. In the case where an order leads to a
number of deliveries, some of the costs arise once per order, and others

once per delivery. As a working guide, the delivery cost may be taken as one half of the ordering cost, except where expensive inspection is involved.

Set-up costs. The request from the stock control clerk goes to the scheduling section of the production control department, where it is embodied in the future programme for the shop concerned, and suitable shop documents are prepared. These are issued to the shop, where any necessary setting up of the machines is done, and the instructions are clarified if this is needed. The cost of setting up a machine itself involves a number of factors:

1   The time of the setter
2   The lost productive time of the machine while it is being set up
3   The time of the operator if he has to stand idle while the machine is in the hands of the setter
4   The cost of any materials or parts used or spoiled during a trial and error series of adjustments

Finished parts have to be inspected, and acceptable parts passed to store, where they are put away and their receipt notified to stock control.

Stockout costs. Stockout costs are of two kinds; the costs arising from the stockout itself or the costs of action taken to deal with the situation arising from the stockout.

Certain costs associated with a stockout are independent of the duration or of the extent of the stockout; for example, if production is switched. If a substitute material is used, the cost depends on the amount used, that is on the extent of the stockout. If production is delayed, the duration of the stockout is the dominant factor.

The only satisfactory course is to evaluate either each case or a case typical of a group of cases, and then to decide which is the appropriate measure:

1   Cost per stockout incident
2   Cost per unit out of stock
3   Cost per unit time of stockout
4   Cost per unit time multiplied by units out of stock

Whichever is chosen, the cost must be turned into an annual cost, to make it compatible with the ordering, delivery and inventory-carrying costs, which are all on an annual basis.

Expediting costs. It is the job of expeditors to prevent a stockout if possible by anticipating it or, failing that, to ameliorate its effect by supplying a substitute or by obtaining a supply quickly. A normal reorder-point stock control system will often have an additional monitor level, below the reorder point, at which a warning is given that a potential danger exists, and this warning brings the expeditors into action. The costs of expediting may include the following:

1   Telephone calls
2   Journeys by car or light van to collect items individually
3   Premium charges paid to a supplier to obtain quick delivery
4   Engineering costs if the use of substitutes requires this
5   The costs of changing order quantities or the supplier

Overall holding cost

The table below gives representative values for all the factors of holding costs:

Cost of money tied up	10%
Storage	3%
Prevention of deterioration	1%
Damage	1%
Pilferage	small
Obsolescence	5%
Insurance	1%
Total	21%

The decisions made in stock control, while dependent on the cost of holding inventory, are not very sensitive to small changes in that cost, so that any value between 20 and 25% may be used without serious error.

Part Five
Working Capital in Export Selling

———————————— 12 ————————————

Management of Export Finance

Funds for export

In many sections of industry success in selling overseas depends on the exporter's willingness to grant extended credit terms to the customers. It is possible to insure about 95 per cent of the risk through ECGD, and the cost of this insurance needs to be added to the expense of the sales when estimating profits and fixing selling prices.

If the customers agree to pay by means of bills of exchange, this brings an extra item into the list of working capital under the title "bills receivable." This is in reality a subdivision of the heading "debtors" but it is kept separate because of the legal differences between a debtor and a bill receivable.

	BEFORE	AFTER
	making export sale of £70 from stock which had cost £20	
Stock	60	40
Bills receivable		70
Debtors	30	30
	90	140
less creditors	20	20
	70	120

FIGURE 12:1   BILLS OF EXCHANGE IN WORKING CAPITAL

In Figure 12:1, there has been a big increase in the working capital and if export selling is repeated regularly whilst the bills receivable remain outstanding on average for a much longer period than ordinary UK debtors, the increase is likely to be permanent.

As with home trade, it is of course possible to find additional funds by discounting on the money market Bills of Exchange drawn on overseas buyers. Obviously the exporter must pay such discount charges as they arise, but these can usually be included in the make-up of the export selling price. This brings out the special importance of the ECGD policy, because concurrent with such a policy ECGD will usually offer its guarantee to the exporter's bankers. This guarantee enables the bank to advance funds additionally to any normal over-drafts arrangements and usually at a marginally lower rate.

The export sales division will have helped the working capital, or least will have avoided embarrassing it, through:

1 Making the sale subject to a bill of exchange rather than merely deferred payment.

2 Insuring the deal with ECGD and covering the insurance cost in the price charged to the customer.

Foreign currency borrowings

The financial scene is constantly changing, particularly when exchange rates are in disequilibrium, and it is worth keeping in touch and looking out for profitable opportunities. 1968 and 1969 saw the appearance and disappearance of "third-country financing" (loans at low rates backed by the West German Bundesbank) and "back-to-back" loans. These are arrangements under which, for example, a US company and a UK company agree to make equivalent loans to one another's subsidiaries in the other country. This type of facility may become popular again if relative availability of credit, interest rates, and ex-change risks make them simultaneously attractive to both sides. Some of these deals are, however, medium rather than short term.

Straightforward foreign currency borrowings, for example in Euro-dollars, D-marks or Swiss francs, are probably a permanent part of the scene, but since early 1971 they are no longer generally available for domestic use in the UK. They are still useful for financing overseas subsidiaries, and sometimes for financing exports (see pages 119–20).

Acceptance credits

Acceptance credits are often used as a general alternative to domestic overdrafts, but they must normally be covered either by export debtors or metals and materials and are often used to finance exports.

They are another form of borrowing from the banking system, but with these differences from overdrafts (which are discussed in Chapter 5):

1 They are basically credits raised on the strength of accommodation bills accepted by an "acceptance house" for a term, for example 90 days, with or without days of grace. They cannot, without penalty, be repaid earlier or later. They can, however, be drawn for a variety of periods like 60, 90 or 120 days. By drawing them so as to mature at (say) fifteen-day intervals, we can turn the tap up, down, on or off at those intervals. Nevertheless, acceptance credits are less flexible than overdrafts.

2 It takes at least two working days to get a bundle of bills ready from decision to draw to receipt of the cash proceeds. There is a logistic cost involved in getting the bills prepared and drawn.

3 The banks find acceptance credits a very convenient form of finance. A facility is usually shared among six to twelve banks who in their turn are free to discount the bills in the discount market according to their day-to-day liquidity position. The *banks* therefore find acceptance credits more flexible than overdrafts.

4 The cost depends on the discount market; it is normally, but by no means always, higher than the cost of overdrafts. The discount charges are borne at the time of drawing, so that the effective cost is a little higher than the apparent cost (when compared with overdrafts), and of course the cost is fixed for the tenor of each bill, irrespective of whether the base rates of the clearing banks go up or down in the meantime.

Foreign currency invoicing

The usefulness of this in terms of financial rather than commercial or marketing considerations depends on relative interest levels in different industrial countries.

Suppose £10 000 worth of goods have been sold to a German customer for payment in six months' time, at a time when short-term D-mark borrowings are cheaper than sterling. It is then arranged to invoice the customer in D-marks, at a price of DM83 000, instead of £10 000. DM83 000 can be borrowed from a bank at a cost below the overdraft rate. This is because it has been assumed DM interest rates are lower.

These D-marks can be sold spot for sterling. The result is that sterling has been received immediately. In six months' time the D-mark repayment can be met out of the payment due from the German customer, and the interest cost is less than the cost of borrowing sterling in London.

This operation is advantageous only if the interest saving is enough to cover the exchange margins charged on conversion. There is no exchange risk more than there would be if the goods were invoiced in sterling. If it is expected that D-marks will be revalued during the next six months, it might pay to invoice in D-marks and carry the credit on the sterling overdraft, but this would for the same reason not suit the German customer.

It would probably be better and safer to draw a 180-day bill on the customer for the DM83 000, and in some circumstances this could make the operation more attractive, for the bank, for example, if there were a market in which the bank could discount the bill. In that case the bank might be willing to cut its rate for the business.

The D-mark borrowing can be arranged with any bank in London, often with London branches of US or European banks.

The operation can be particularly convenient and attractive if the customer is a subsidiary and if there is a steady volume of sales to that subsidiary which needs financing for the period taken by the subsidiary to sell and collect cash from its customers.

Management of Export Debtors

Control of export debtors

The basic principles of sound initial credit sanction, regular survey of credit limits and a disciplined but flexible collection procedure remain the same as for the domestic market. There are, however, some special factors which should be borne in mind and a particular technology necessary.

First of all the simple distance factor.

For those overseas clients, who are not seen personally, it is necessary to rely upon information which cannot easily be verified personally. For that reason it is even more important to build up a credit dossier from a number of sources. The Department of Trade and Industry through the commercial secretaries in UK embassies will often help with customer information.

It will not give a credit report as such but it will tell something of the client's repute in the marketplace, size and situation of premises, agencies held and so on. The chambers of commerce are helpful in these matters too and it should not be forgotten that the trade reference is available internationally as well as in the domestic market.

The payment risk for exports is not concerned solely however with the client's character, capital and capacity. It is also very largely conditioned by the economic condition of the buying country. Our exports represent other countries' imports and imports require the necessary foreign exchange to be available before they can be paid for. In many countries of the world the exchange available for the payment of imports is allocated by the issue of import licences and where such a licence is necessary the credit manager would be wise to ensure that he has its number and expiry date before approving the order for dispatch. Some countries are very reliant upon one main source of exchange earnings, particularly in the prime producing countries and any temporary impediment to that source can mean long exchange delays— thus a drought in the Sudan can mean the loss of a cotton crop, Sudan's staple source of sterling. Then too a coup d'état or sudden change of government can bring a new ideology to a country's import programme, a change of import emphasis from East to West or vice versa. In any event these matters all affect in one degree or another the payment risk and the manager of export receivables must therefore keep very much abreast of international economic and political events.

With regard to world economics the banks provide free most excellent and regular economic surveys of most countries, particularly those in which they have special interests. Both Barclays Bank and Swiss Bank Corporation publish useful guides to the payment risks abroad and both are free on application.

Methods of payment

It is not usual for a debtor to pay by cheque on his own bank, as it would be in the domestic market; instead there are other methods of payment, all of them using in one form or another the operations of the international banks.

Cash with order. If the customer is believed to have no substance or his country is in the middle of a revolution and his money is required before shipment, he will in all probability arrange a banker's transfer. This means that he will tell his bank to remit to their UK correspondent the amount concerned under advice to, or to the credit of, the exporter's account. The UK correspondent of the customer's bankers on receipt of the instructions advise and/or credit the exporter accordingly and the value is received. No actual payment instrument passes, the whole thing is done by bookkeeping entries in the books of the banks in the chain. Alternatively the customer will ask his bank to send the exporter its draft for the amount concerned on a UK bank. This is in effect a banker's cheque made out in the exporter's favour and can be dealt with on receipt as such.

Letter of credit. Again the exporter wants his credit risk secured but the customer wants also to ensure that the supply side of the bargain is satisfactory. In these circumstances a documentary letter of credit should be requested. The one most commonly used, because it is the "safest" is one known as confirmed and irrevocable. The client wishing to open such a credit instructs his local bank accordingly. That bank will in turn inform its UK correspondent bank and advise the exporter of the value of the credit and any conditions. Once opened, the credit cannot be revoked before expiry by the foreign bank and the confirmation of the UK bank means that even if the foreign bank goes into liquidation during the validity of the credit, the UK bank will pay providing the exporter meets the conditions of the credit and that the documents are in order when presented. What then are those all important conditions as set out in the advice of a confirmed irrevocable letter of credit? The main ones are as follows:

1 That the documents must be presented on or before close of business on the credit's expiry date.

2 That shipment must be made on or before a specific date or dates that will enable condition 1 to be met.

3 That goods are shipped exactly as specified in the credit as to description, quantity, origin, price, etc.

4 That the method of dispatch shall be as set out in the credit—it is of no use trying to catch up on a late delivery by sending air freight when the credit calls for shipment by boat—the bank would not pay out.

5 That all the documents asked for are submitted exactly as specified.

The terms of a documentary letter of credit can be amended only by the overseas client so that any amendments the exporter needs in order to make compliance practical for him, must be the subject of communication between him and his buyer. Certainly the UK paying bank can do nothing about varying the terms. All it can do if presentation does not comply with the terms and conditions is to decide whether or not to accept the exporter's guarantee for the discrepancy. Such a guarantee given by the exporter means of course, that he has lost his security in the credit since the buyer can if he wishes claim that the credit terms were not met and abrogate the contract.

Cash on delivery. There is sometimes confusion regarding the use of this particular phrase. In its usually accepted sense, COD means the seller will dispatch his goods via the Post Office, who will deliver them to the buyer's address but will collect the invoiced value before surrendering the goods to the buyer. This is seldom, if ever, the case in overseas markets. Here it is usually the case that on arrival of the parcel the overseas Post Office will advise the customer that it is available for collection against payment of the total charge.

If the client for any reason has lost interest in the deal or is, if only temporarily, short of money, the parcel will wait gathering dust on the shelf of that far off Post Office. Meantime protracted correspondence with the UK Post Office brings no satisfaction. In any event, the overseas COD service is slow in terms of overall collection time and we can reckon to be out of our money for at least six weeks, with the attendant risk that our client may never take up the goods, necessitating their return, possibly damaged.

The bill of exchange is described in the Bills of Exchange Act very lucidly as: "an unconditional order in writing, addressed by one person to another, signed by the person giving it, requiring the person to whom it is addressed to pay on demand or at a fixed or determinable future time, a sum certain in money to or to the order of a specified person, or to bearer."

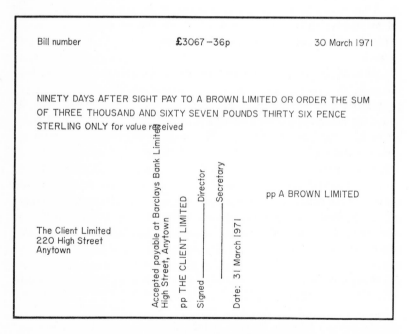

FIGURE 13:1   BILL OF EXCHANGE

This very clear piece of legal drafting has never needed amendment and results in bills of exchange being a main source of the financing of trade both home and export.

For financing and credit purposes a usance or time bill is used which has a period of time or "tenor" between the time the drawee sees it for the first time and the date on which he has to pay its value. The procedure is very broadly as follows.

A debtor may agree with his creditor that the amount to be paid shall be covered by a bill of exchange. Against such an agreement the creditor, possibly in the shape of the credit manager, will draw a bill of exchange on the debtor for the amount and time agreed upon. On receipt or presentation the debtor will add his acceptance by writing across the face of the bill the place where it becomes payable at maturity or due date and adding his signature and capacity of office (see Figure 13:1). The bill is then returned to the creditors.

On the home or domestic market it is the time bill that is normally drawn by a creditor since it is a form of financial accommodation offered by that creditor to his debtor. In the export market it is by no means uncommon to draw what is known as a bill at sight or sight draft. Such a bill is worded "*At sight* pay to the order of . . ." and so on, and cannot of course be "accepted" by the drawee who must pay the face value on presentation—that is, sighting.

In the home market the bill of exchange is known as a "clean" bill simply because it is drawn for an agreed amount and sent to the drawee usually with only a covering letter. For export it is the almost universal practice to use what is known as the documentary bill. As will be explained later, the export of goods entails the use of many documents which in most cases are essential for the buyer or his agent to clear the goods through customs on arrival.

Because of their importance to the buyer these documents are attached to the bill of exchange and released to the buyer only when the conditions of the bill have been met—that is, a sight bill paid or a time bill accepted—hence the expression documentary bill. The exporter's bank becomes the collecting agent in collaboration with its "correspondent" bank in the town on which the bill is drawn. From the security angle, the advantage of the documentary bill will be obvious—broadly the client can get the documents he needs to clear his goods only when he has met or accepted the bill.

In the pre-war and immediate post-war years, the bill of exchange was almost always used as the medium of payment for exports from Britain very largely because Britain has a developed sophisticated bill market. This was not so in many continental and other countries who shipped their goods *"open account"* with its greater attendant risk and advantage to the overseas buyer. To compete, many UK exporters departed from their established bill practice and also moved to open account facilities and for a number of years the documentary bill of exchange suffered a decline in popularity. However, its advantages asserted themselves and over the last few years it has again been increasingly used as the principal payment instrument for international trade not only by UK exporters but also by those on the Continent and North America.

A documentary usance or time bill of exchange carries the usual credit risk of non-payment at maturity and in some countries, particularly in South America, such a dishonoured bill must be protested with a notary public before it can be held up legally as good evidence of debt. The collecting bank requires instructions from the exporter as to whether the bill if dishonoured should be "protested" and these must be given at the time the bill is sent for collection since "protest" if necessary must be done quickly by the local bank in the buyer's country. Protesting a bill is, however, quite an expensive business and if the client has withheld settlement for what he considers to be a valid dispute with his creditor, "protest" could well mean the loss of a good client. The credit manager will be wise therefore to give "protest" some considerable thought and if in doubt to seek the advice of his bankers. It is often said by the uninitiated that a documentary sight draft carries no credit risk. Theoretically this is true since the collecting bank should not hand over the documents of title to the buyer until payment of the bill has been made. In practice some banks will hand over the documents against a verbal understanding or guarantee.

This is particularly so where the exporter at his buyer's request has arranged for the local collecting bank to be the same one as the buyer uses for his other business. Thus the local bank manager finds himself as agent for the exporter's bank and also acting in the interests of his own customer. If the local bank does part with the documents and payment is not forthcoming then of course, it can be held liable.

It is much more often the case that, when the goods arrive, the buyer has not the cash available to pay for them and after numerous reports back to the exporter's bank and further attempts to present the documents for payment, there is nothing left but to ask the exporter to arrange for the return of the goods. The normal average collection time for a sight bill paid promptly is four to six weeks overall but delays of two to three months and more are not uncommon. It will be seen therefore that within the truism "the longer the credit the bigger the risk" a documentary sight bill does indeed carry a very definite risk not only of non-payment but of the costs of getting the goods back, probably damaged.

Open account. To ship on these terms means quite simply that an exporter sends the invoice and documents direct to the overseas buyer or his agent and expects payment to be made on an agreed due date. There is no banker acting as intermediary or collecting agent and the exporter is completely in the hands of his buyer as regards a proper settlement. In a multiple shipment, that is one consisting of a number of invoices on the same buyer, that buyer on open account terms can select the invoices he chooses to pay—had the total multiple consignment been covered by a bill of exchange for the total amount, the buyer would have had no such choice. When the buyer wants to settle the account he will in all probability ask his bankers to remit by air-mail transfer which is simply a means of inter-bank payments by means of a suitable air-mailed credit advice. On receipt of such an advice the bank in the exporter's country will advise the exporter of its arrival.

In the United Kingdom there are a number of companies acting as merchants or confirming houses. For the practical purposes of the credit manager they offer one great advantage—payment is made in the United Kingdom, usually "cash against documents" or at the end of the month of receipt of the invoice, and the confirming house or merchant assumes the credit risk thereafter on the overseas buyer. Because in most instances such merchants and confirming houses act for the overseas buyer as UK buying agents, it is the overseas buyer who pays the commission on which such export houses live.

Export documentation

Mention has been made of the "documents" or "documents of title" and because the receivables manager must rely much upon their accuracy to get his money, a brief survey of their nature will be useful.

Bill of lading. This is a receipt for the goods from the shipowner— quite an imposing looking document signed by or on behalf of the ship's master. Until a signed copy of the bill of lading is presented on arrival at the port of discharge to the shipping company's agent, that agent will not, as a general rule, release the goods to the importer or buyer. There are exceptions when the bill of lading will be released without presentation of a bill of lading, but only against a form of guarantee acceptable to the shipowner's agents.

Air consignment note. Merely evidence from the airline that the goods have been dispatched on a particular flight—it carries no "title" as such and the goods will be released to the buyer on application at the airport of discharge. Because of the obvious credit risk in the event of doubt about the buyer's credit standing it is often prudent to consign the goods to the overseas collecting bank with instructions that release may be affected only against payment. Such an arrangement should be agreed between the exporter, his buyer and the buyer's bank before the goods are dispatched.

Marine insurance policy or certificate. Issued by the insurers or their brokers in evidence that the goods have been insured against the perils of the voyage and is essential in the event of loss for the buyer to institute his insurance claim.

Combined certificate of value and origin. Required by most Commonwealth countries for the importer to obtain such preferential import duty rates as are left under the remnants of the old Ottawa Agreements. This certificate usually forms a part of the actual export invoice.

Legalised invoice. A copy of the invoice "legalised" by the chamber of commerce as to the authenticity and accuracy of the details given—required only in some overseas markets.

Consular invoice. Similar to a legalised invoice but on an elaborate form issued by the embassy or consulate of the importer in the exporting country. After completion which must comply in every detail with the commercial invoice and import licence, this document will be signed and stamped by the embassy or consulate on payment of a very considerable ad valorem stamp duty.

EFTA Certificate. Required under the regulation of the European Free Trade Area as to value and origin of the goods.

Parcel post receipt. Issued by the Post Office as evidence that the goods have been posted through the mails to the address shown thereon.

The export documents mentioned are "mainstream" and no attempt has been made to explain the legal complexity of each one. Documentation itself will usually be completed by a forwarding agent or department, but its final collation and disposal is a matter of concern for the credit manager since his collection success of the export proceeds is to a large extent dependent upon these documents.

Management of Export Risks

Exchange risk

This can be avoided by selling abroad only in the currency of the exporter's country. Frequently, however, and very naturally, an importer will want to purchase in his own currency and for "commercial" reasons it may be thought necessary to accommodate an overseas buyer in this way. That being so, the credit manager will be faced with the fact that he is unlikely to receive the exact amount as is reflected in his books, simply because the exchange rate used to convert the invoice total in buyer's currency to his own currency for bookkeeping purposes will in all probability change during the interval between booking the invoice and receipt of payment.

The shortfall or excess in amount received can be "written off" to difference on exchange account, but the amount can be minimised by taking a forward view of the rate at the time of receipt of the proceeds and "making up" an internal exchange rate for bookkeeping purposes. More prudently, however, the credit manager, expecting his proceeds in say ninety days' time, will arrange forward cover with his bankers. This means basically that he undertakes to sell or deliver the currency of the invoice total to his banker on a future date. The banker will then take the forward view based upon his own expertise and quote the exporter a forward rate—that is, he guarantees to buy the currency at that rate in ninety days' time. Thus the credit manager can book the invoice at a rate which he knows will entail no loss (or profit if his own currency hardens against that of the importer). Should the importer fail to pay on due date the credit manager will be unable to deliver his currency to his banker and will have to "buy in" an equivalent amount at spot rate and sell it to the bank at the agreed forward rate, at the same time taking up another forward contract for the new expected payment date. Forward contracts are again a complicated topic, but it is hoped that enough has been said to make clear the basic principles.

Insuring the risk

As with his "home" market, consideration should be given to obtaining insurance cover on the risk of non-payment, insolvency or protracted default of the debtor. Insurance companies such as Trade Indemnity offer a variety of policies to cover this form of risk—in some cases tailor-made to suit the particular nature of the insured business. This consideration is even more important in the export market where there are many other risks attendant upon eventual payment, risks sometimes beyond the control of either buyer or seller—war, civil commotion, revocation of an import licence, exchange transfer delays, and so on—that is, the "political risks." These contingencies and more, can be covered along with the "commercial risks" by what is known as an "ECGD policy", arranged either direct with the insurer or through a broker. Export Credit Guarantee Department is part of the Department of Trade & Industry. It operates under a charter which requires that financially it shall break even taking one period of time with another—this means in effect that it has to operate on a proper commercial underwriting basis with an adequate spread of risk. An exporter can select an ECGD policy for what is called short-term credit—that is, up to two years—of two basic types—contracts or shipments. In the first case, the insured is on risk from the date the contract is signed (his manufacturing period and costs are covered) whilst in the second type, the cover commences at the date of shipment. The credit manager selling specially made goods will want and need a "contracts policy" whilst another concerned with mass produced merchandise to no particular customer specification will find the shipment policy sufficient and cheaper.

ECGD normally covers up to 95% of the political and 85% of the commercial (customer's insolvency) risk. 100% cover would leave the exporter with little incentive to exercise care in accepting risks. ECGD vets the credit standing of the foreign buyers it is asked to cover, but the exporter is allowed a "discretionary" limit up to which he may give credit to any one customer, provided that the exporter has proper status information and credit-sanction routines of his own.

ECGD's main concern is the political, not the insolvency risk. If a whole country like Brazil, Turkey or Indonesia cannot meet its payments any more, ECGD stands to suffer a heavily concentrated loss. That is why ECGD normally requires an exporter to cover his whole world turnover, not just sales to risky countries. Countries are graded as *A*, *B*, *C* or *D* risks and premium rates vary principally according to these gradings. Occasionally, when the underwriters of ECGD feel that for any one country the "credit ceiling" has been reached, cover for that country will be removed.

Once ECGD has accepted a proposal and issued its policy, the day-to-day operation of the policy is neither onerous nor difficult. Premium rates have been reduced over the years and are very reasonable and competitive. It should not be prohibitive to recover the premium cost in export prices. In any case, the cost is less than the provision against bad export debts that exporters would otherwise have to create against this risky part of the portfolio of debtors.

ECGD's export financing aids

ECGD not only insures export credit risks, but also eases the burden of financing export debtors. There are several schemes for this, and in varying degrees they confer some or all of the following benefits on the exporter:

1 Access to additional finance from banks
2 Cheaper interest cost
3 Fixed interest cost, thus removing uncertainty
4 Removing the debtor from the balance sheet altogether, thus improving the exporter's liquidity.

Under all the schemes, the bank that finances the export debt enjoys an unconditional guarantee from ECGD against the risk of non-payment by the overseas customer.

The schemes differ in that under some of them the bank lends its money to the exporter (who carries the advance as a liability on his balance sheet), under some the bank "buys" the debt from the exporter without recourse, and under some the bank lends direct to the overseas buyer, who pays the exporter cash.

Under all the schemes, ECGD (not the bank) retains recourse against the exporter:

1   To the extent of the uninsured proportion of the credit risk (normally 15% for insolvency, 5% for political risks).
2   In the event that the customer's non-payment turns out to be due to a risk not covered by ECGD, which in practice means a dispute about the exporter's performance of his contract.

The schemes are more fully summarised in the Board of Trade Export Handbook No. 2 (4th edition). Here is a brief summary:

Comprehensive bill guarantees. For short-term credits. The bank finances the bills of exchange without recourse and charges interest at Bank Rate.

Comprehensive open account guarantees. Like comprehensive bill guarantees, but applicable where the debt is not represented by bills of exchange or promissory notes. The finance is with recourse to the exporter, who therefore is the bank's debtor.

Specific guarantees to banks. For larger contracts, where the credit period extends to at least two years. Finance is without recourse, and interest is at the fixed export rate ($6\frac{1}{2}$% since October 1971).

Financial guarantees. For major projects, minimum £2 million (£1 million for ships) Bank lends to foreign buyer, who pays exporter cash. Credit periods can extend up to 15 years after contract date.

Buyer credit. Like financial guarantees, but for smaller projects with credits of two to five years, and simpler documentation. These are sometimes available for "lines of credit" open to foreign governments who are then free to shop around among UK exporters. Under financial guarantees and buyer credits, the overseas customer is charged the special export rate of interest ($6\frac{1}{2}$% since October 1971).

Exchange control regulations

The export credit manager must be aware of the requirements of the Exchange Control Act 1947 as they relate to getting paid for goods shipped abroad and the disposal of any foreign currencies so earned. Within the context of this chapter it is sufficient to say that for United Kingdom exchange control purposes the world is divided into two main monetary areas—the sterling area and the external account area. Very broadly, without permission from the Bank of England, it is not permitted to export to a country of the external account area and get paid from a country in the sterling area unless the funds are specially designated as external account sterling. Thus, if a Jamaican customer specifies delivery to New York (external account area) but to invoice Kingston, Jamaica (sterling area) written confirmation is needed that payment to the UK will come from an external account, if not, the matter must be referred to the Bank of England (exchange control) through the exporter's own bankers before shipment is made.

Part Six
Appendices

APPENDIX 1

Dealing with a Surplus of Liquidity

Where a company is in the unusual position of having more cash than it is currently needing so that cash stands idle in the bank account, there may be opportunities for making extra profits by skilful deployment of those resources.

The surplus should not be left stagnant in the current account but should be invested on a short-term basis for the most favourable terms available. The larger the amount involved, the more worthwhile it is to make the arrangements even for a very short period.

If the surplus is only temporary

In a small company £5000 surplus for four weeks invested at 5% per annum would earn £20 which amply repays the trouble of making the transfer to a bank deposit account. In a much larger company having the same amount of £5000 with opportunity to earn £20 might look trivial to executives accustomed to turnover figures quoted in hundreds of thousands, but it is still bearing the same relationship to earnings of the staff needed to look after the transfer.

To gain the full benefit of the deposit account interest it is necessary to give seven days' notice of withdrawal and this is where the accuracy of the forecasting system shows its value.

Placing the funds in short-term investments is the most obvious course of action. However, other ideas involving management action on the part of the various executives may be worked out and in some cases could prove more lucrative than a short-term investment. Also these alternative actions may be useful in avoiding shortfall directions (see Appendix 2) whereas short-term investments would be ineffective for this purpose.

1 Buy in extra supplies of raw material. This could be attractive if the current market price for the material appears unusually low. However, commodity markets are always treacherous and the expectation that today's price because it is less than the average price of the past two years is just going through a temporary drop could prove mistaken. The purchasing officer's skill and his knowledge of the market must be exercised to cut down the element of speculation.

Buying larger quantities to increase stocks may also bring a price reduction because bulk orders are being placed.

Two particular dangers in this plan are the costs of actually storing the extra material and the danger it could deteriorate or go out of fashion before being needed. The benefits must be compared to these assets and the company should never go to extremes with holding large stocks.

2 Invest more in personnel. Engage trainees in both the factory and the management division. Pay for their training; let these trainees relieve longer serving staff who can then go forward for advanced training refresher courses, management seminars and other programmes for improving their skills.

3 Seek special discount from suppliers in return for paying promptly. Many companies are desperately short of liquid funds and will jump at the chance of having a customer pay his account by return of post.

If the surplus is expected to last for a longer period

For some companies a surplus of cash may endure for a comparatively long period. This may be because:

1 Trade is depressed. However, the duration of this cannot be foreseen so the review of short-term investments must constantly be checked and kept on the very short basis for which bank deposit account is ideally suited, or

2 It may be because funds are being stored in readiness for some big commitment in one or two years' time when a new factory will be put into use.

These slightly longer times, with a reasonably definite duration, give some scope for finding more lucrative temporary investments. Loans to local corporations are one of the best safe outlets with a good rate of interest and a fixed time for repayment. Some financial companies offer higher returns for one- or two-year advances, but the lender must accept some risk that the company may not meet the agreed repayment time, or in extreme cases may fail entirely. High returns and complete safety are incompatible.

Care should be taken to avoid making temporary investments in quoted shares. During long spells the stock exchange prices may be steadily increasing which gives the appearance of an excellent capital gain, boosting the modest annual yield on the shares, but the weakness lies in the risk that the share price may fall sharply just at the time this company is anxious to sell. Investment in quoted shares is essentially for those who are looking for long-term plans and are certain not to be needing to sell at one particular date which might prove inconvenient.

Among other opportunities which may be considered by management facing a persistent or permanent surplus of working capital are the following:

1 Offer customers an extension of credit terms in return for an interest payment. This needs to be done with great care because the risk of bad debts will multiply in a geometric progression as the customers are allowed longer for paying their accounts. This risk often outweighs the cash advantage of either the interest added to the accounts or the fact of selling more to customers who are attracted to buy because of the extension of payment time.

2 Transfer funds from liquid into fixed assets. Whereas the leasing of fixed assets is a means of releasing funds to augment working capital, the reverse process of purchasing fixed assets will soak up the working capital. It has the advantage that once the assets have been bought an unforeseen downturn in sales and profits is less damaging to the company. If large rents are being paid for assets on lease, this regular commitment can be embarrassing when trading income is suddenly curtailed. The purchase of fixed assets when funds are plentiful spells long-term security.

3 Turn some resources to new small trial projects. These may include research and development into new products and new methods of production.

4 Spend in extending into new markets to cut down the long-term dependence on the existing markets. Market development is usually slow and expensive so the ideal time to do it is when the company is prosperous. Without the development there is a risk that existing markets will shrink and the company will be hit by falling sales.

5 Make trade investments in other companies to establish stronger relationships. This may be vertical integration with customers and suppliers to safeguard outlets and the flow of raw material, or it may be horizontal integration with companies carrying on the same line of business thus cutting down competition or buying a way into new markets or new production facilities.

Liquidity
and Shortfall Directions

In certain specific circumstances a surplus of liquidity can result in an increased tax liability. Until April 1973, when the corporation tax rules are due for drastic revision, the more successful private limited companies may live under a threat of shortfall direction. This is a tax penalty imposed as punishment for failing to pay out the required standard proportion of their net after-tax profits as dividend. It falls:

1   On the company in the shape of a demand to hand over the same income tax that it would have needed to deduct if it had in fact paid out the larger dividends
2   On the individual shareholders who must pay surtax as if they had in fact received the full gross dividend. In effect, they are paying surtax on an imaginary dividend

The required standard dividend is the lower of:

1   60% of the trading income plus 100% of investment income remaining after paying corporation tax
2   Such amount as could be paid out without prejudicing the company's financial position

The onus falls on the company for improving the situation in 2 above. The double attractions of not declaring dividends are, of course:

1   The company retains the use of the funds to finance its expansion

2   The income tax and surtax payable by the shareholders is avoided, unless there is a shortfall direction

---

Example

FIRST COMPANY

	BEFORE PAYING DIVIDEND		AFTER PAYING DIVIDEND OF £10 000	
	£'000		£'000	
Fixed assets		60		60
Current assets stock	30		30	
debtors	50	80	50	80
less current liabilities		30 50		40 40
		110		100

Current ratio 80/30 = 2.6:1   80/40 = 2:1

liquid ratio   50/30 = 1.6:1   50/40 = 1.25:1

SECOND COMPANY

	BEFORE PAYING DIVIDEND		AFTER PAYING DIVIDEND OF £10,000	
	£'000		£'000	
Fixed assets		60		60
Current assets stock	80		80	
debtors	30	110	30	110
less current liabilities		60 50		70 40
		110		100

Current ratio 110/60 = 1.8:1   110/70 = 1.5:1
liquid ratio   30/60 = 0.5:1   30/70 = 0.4:1

The first company has a fairly good current ratio before paying its dividend but a moderately decent liquid ratio. After paying the dividend its liquid ratio has worsened which is due to having withdrawn cash from the business to send to the shareholders. However, the liquid ratio is still fairly satisfactory and the directors will have been faced with a shortfall direction if they had decided against declaring the dividend.

In the second company there is an identical total of working capital but there are more stocks and more debtors offset by more creditors. The effect has been to cut back the current and liquid ratios and the liquid ratio in particular is in a hazardous position. Only the forbearance of the creditors in not pressing for payment is enabling the company to keep going.

Therefore it would be positively dangerous to declare the dividend as it would make the liquid ratio even more precarious. The directors would be well placed to resist any threat of a shortfall direction if they refused to declare a dividend.

The special connection with working capital becomes obvious when the two companies are compared with one another. The one which has reversed the normal objectives of keeping stock, debtors and creditors as low as possible has been enabled to withhold its dividend safely.

However, great care is needed in following such a policy. Holding large stocks is expensive and carries the extra risk that the stock may prove unsaleable for one of many possible reasons. Allowing the customers to run up large overdue accounts is dangerous because it multiplies the risks of bad debts as well as being costly. Only rarely is it possible to win a concession of delayed payment terms for suppliers' accounts.

Therefore the expansion of current assets and liabilities not matched by an increase in permanent funds is not attractive merely as a tax avoidance device. Saving tax through missing the shortfall direction must be merely an incidental bonus, whilst the real object of the exercise is to increase profit through:

1   Having a better selection of stock to offer customers
2   Agreeing longer settlement terms for selected customers who might otherwise be unwilling to buy from this source

Index